Out of Many Faiths

OUR
COMPELLING
INTERESTS

Earl Lewis and Nancy Cantor, Series Editors

Other books in this series:

Scott E. Page,
The Diversity Bonus: How Great Teams Pay Off in the Knowledge Economy
Earl Lewis and Nancy Cantor, editors,
Our Compelling Interests: The Value of Diversity for Democracy and a Prosperous Society

Out of Many Faiths

Religious Diversity and the American Promise

Eboo Patel

PRINCETON UNIVERSITY PRESS
Princeton and Oxford

Copyright © 2018 by Princeton University Press

Requests for permission to reproduce material from this work should be sent to permissions@press.princeton.edu

Published by Princeton University Press
41 William Street, Princeton, New Jersey 08540
6 Oxford Street, Woodstock, Oxfordshire OX20 1TR
press.princeton.edu

All Rights Reserved

Library of Congress Control Number: 2018943925
ISBN 978-0-691-18272-8

British Library Cataloging-in-Publication Data is available

Editorial: Eric Crahan and Pamela Weidman
Production Editorial: Karen Carter
Jacket Design: Faceout Studio, Derek Thornton
Jacket Art: Courtesy of Shutterstock
Production: Jacqueline Poirier
Publicity: Julia Haav
Copyeditor: Ashley Moore

This book has been composed in Arno and Futura

Printed on acid-free paper. ∞

Printed in the United States of America

10 9 8 7 6 5 4 3 2 1

There is but one destiny . . . left for us, and that is to make ourselves, and be made by others a part of the American people in every sense of the word.

—FREDERICK DOUGLASS

Contents

Acknowledgments

In the spring of 2016, I received a surprise phone call from my friend Nancy Cantor, Chancellor of Rutgers University in Newark. She and Earl Lewis were co-editors of an important new book series about diversity in American life called Our Compelling Interests, and they wanted me to be the principal author of the volume on religion.

"Nancy, I just finished a book," I said. "I'm not sure I have the energy to start another one right away."

"The series is a partnership between the Andrew Mellon Foundation and Princeton University Press, and we believe it can play a critical role in helping America positively engage the challenges and opportunities of our growing diversity."

How was I going to say no to that?

I'm enormously grateful to Nancy and Earl for electing to include a volume on religion in a series on diversity (it's a category that is too often ignored in identity conversations), and for selecting me to be the principal author. I'm also grateful to the authors of the three excellent commentaries included in the volume: Robert Jones, John Inazu, and Laurie Patton.

I truly enjoyed working with Doreen Tinajero and Makeba Morgan Hill at the Mellon Foundation. The entire Our Compelling Interests series relies on their excellent behind-the-scenes work. The staff of the Mellon Foundation and the Advisory Board for the series made useful comments on the manuscript. Many thanks to them. Similar gratitude is due the staff at Princeton University Press, particularly Eric Crahan.

Special thanks to several American Muslim friends who read and offered comments on the sections about our faith community: Alia Bilal, Haroon Mogul, Kashif Shaikh, Jenan Mohajir, Rami Nashashibi, and Zeenat Rahman. I am proud to be building American Islam with you.

A big thank you to the board and staff at Interfaith Youth Core, who gave me the time and space to work on this book amid a full-to-bursting program schedule. Special thanks to Mesha Arant and Teri Simon at IFYC, who helped with research, editing, and preparing the manuscript for publication.

And finally, to my wonderful family—parents and brother, wife and kids—who encourage me even when it goes against some of their most compelling interests. As my wife Shehnaz wisely notes, "Yes, you're moody when you're writing a book, but you're worse when you've got a book in your head that you're not writing."

Introduction

Earl Lewis and Nancy Cantor

Every Mother's Day at the New Jersey Performing Arts Center in Newark, New Jersey, the Alvin Ailey Dance Company performs *Revelations* to a packed audience of families, from children to senior citizens, as diverse a crowd as one can conjure—peoples of all hues, heritages, faiths, dress, and languages. Strongly identified with the particulars of the Christian spiritual tradition, the dance invoked a message that moved members of multiple faith traditions. There are universal elements to the story. There are those who see in it an affirmation of a particular struggle for civil rights, and those who identify with it from a less personally direct lineage but find its call to humanity and the human spirit compelling nonetheless. It feels like America at its best, and the moment is decidedly strengthened by the variety of personal histories in the room, as it is also by the commonality of the experience of uplift. There is always a loud and resoundingly prolonged standing ovation, as the audience holds out the hope that the moment of collective affirmation will last. Indeed, those are the moments that we want to last, in which diversity contributes powerfully to the strength of community. And although it surely isn't only a day a year that this is evident, it does seem that there are precious few demonstrations these days of what some might say is the distinctly American ethos, *E pluribus unum*.

The Fraying of *E pluribus unum* and the Bonds of Empathetic Citizenship

Arguably, we live in a time comparable to many of the most strained periods in our national history. It is a time when the human bonds of empathetic citizenship—the openness to see value in others different from oneself and the concomitant responsibility for bridging those differences to create an interdependent whole—are deeply frayed. This fraying of the bonds of citizenship imperils the fabric of democracy itself, as we have seen from sea to shining sea. Who, after all, would have predicted that in the twenty-first century the signs, symbols, and rhetoric of the Nazi era would be on public display in crowds marching on a college campus in Charlottesville, Virginia, chanting, "Jews won't replace us" and "Blood and soil"? What do we say when nooses appear overnight on the National Mall in Washington, DC, directed especially at the Smithsonian's National Museum of African American History and Culture?

Where do we situate religion in this recurring clash of visions? Have we regressed to another bleak period of our national history, when we created Japanese American internment camps on our own soil in reaction to the bombing of Pearl Harbor? Following that playbook, will we lock up Muslim Americans, our neighbors in cities and towns across America, painting all with the brush of a threat from violent extremism? How do we reconcile the reluctance to label some violent acts of hate committed by white Christians (adhering to supremacist ideology) as domestic terrorism, on the one hand, with the speed with which we make that connection to hateful acts committed by other citizens but in the name of Islam, on the other?[1] Is it purely accidental that half a century after the bombing of children in a Birmingham church in 1963, a hate-filled supremacist murders nine people in a prayer service at Emanuel African Methodist Episcopal Church in Charleston, South Carolina, in 2015? Or is there something about the theology of hate that is more fully comprehended in the presence of the theology of inclusion?[2] Have we moved on so little from our racist, xenophobic, and religiously exclusionary past and progressed so little in expanding the narrative of who is American, even as the facts of our diversity become more pronounced and our aspirations for pluralism march resoundingly forward?

Even though some may express fear, our increasing diversity is indisputable. How we define and leverage diversity for the common good is not. It is against the backdrop of threats to social connectedness, to civic democracy, to moral neighborliness, that this book series considers the myriad dimensions of our compelling interests.[3] We ask how we move beyond our worst history: genocide against Native Americans; Atlantic slavery and the long path traveled toward enfranchisement of African Americans; religious bigotry and exclusion. We question, even as we appear reluctant to relinquish this hibernating bigotry,[4] what new vision is to be crafted of a diverse, pluralistic society where civil rights and generous civic behavior go hand in hand, where diversity and democracy mix well, as they also sometimes have in our history.[5] We wonder how we will flourish as a nation without the full participation of our ever more diverse populace and the diversity bonus that such engagement brings to our knowledge economy, as well as to the classrooms that prepare our talent, the halls of government that make our policies, and the places of innovation that crisscross our communities.[6]

Expanding the American Civic Religious Narrative

In this volume, we turn to what has been foundational to our national identity, emblazoned in our initiating documents as the freedom of religion and the establishment of a government embracing our people's many faiths and traditions. We tackle what an expanded, inclusive, but not homogenized civil religious narrative might be in this twenty-first-century America, as Eboo Patel frames the central dilemma of our religiously and ethnically diverse nation. We start with the basic premise of his analysis, that the vibrancy of civic life is enhanced by religious participation and therefore by tolerance for religious diversity in its broadest sense. As his section and the commentaries in this volume detail, there is no guarantee that we are up to the challenge of matching religious diversity and civic tolerance. On the contrary, there is every reason to wonder whether the American democratic project, built on a promise of religious diversity and freedom amid a reality of expectations of assimilation, can stretch and evolve sufficiently to reap the benefits of the insights and talents of new communities of faith in our midst.

The challenge posed by the demographic and religious map of America today may well tax the limits of an expanded embrace, as religion mixes once again with race and ethnicity and homeland, perhaps in ways less palatable to many than in the past. As both Patel and Robert P. Jones explicate, while the journeys into the fold of the American civic religious tradition may not always have been smooth, the assimilation of Catholic and Jewish immigrants, among others, was accomplished over time both by stretching the definition of whiteness and simultaneously by moving the prevalent religious narrative (from Anglo-Saxon Protestant) to an expanded Judeo-Christian one. Today this inclusiveness may be harder to achieve. In fact, the Cold War created a need for a rewrite of America's religious narrative. If the Soviet Union and China were godless, America was godly. This rewrite enabled the pivot from a narrative about Anglo-Saxon Protestants to one of a Judeo-Christian community. With growing (though still proportionately small) numbers of Americans identifying as Muslim (with many origins, including African Americans) and an increasingly pervasive political landscape of Islamophobia and American nationalism, American Muslims, some of whose families have been here for decades, if not centuries, as Patel ironically points out, test both the dominance of whiteness and the centrality of Christianity (even in its adapted version, where the symbols and language of faith are imported into a somewhat neutered public civic sphere). And the threat of losing predominance, of being displaced, as Jones characterizes it, is made worse for some by the growing populations of religiously unaffiliated Americans, particularly in younger generations. The threat of the unaffiliated is only exacerbated, as John Inazu's commentary delineates, as many push for a set of policies and laws that protect rights and enforce responsibilities that some see as threatening religious freedom (if not religion itself), from contraception coverage to transgender bathroom choice. This growing divide is bolstered no doubt also by a prevalent narrative that lays the economic losses of rural white Christians at the feet of the largely metropolitan, and less Christian or less religiously identified, "elite," who are said to welcome foreigners and not to care about the loss of American jobs to globalization.

This mix of exclusionary racial and religious sentiments with antiglobal paranoia, while certainly not new in our nation's history, is finding new life in a range of public debates, from affirmative action to immigration, and a substantial uptick in acts of vandalism and violence in places of worship and community centers, especially those hosting Jews or Muslims. Patel poignantly documents, in telling the story of American Muslims, how they have become an all-encompassing blank screen on which to project anger and resentment about race, immigration, national security, and religion. At their core, these anti-Muslim expressions, often dragging in other minority identities in the process, belie a fear of the erosion of some foundational American identity and way of life—an existential threat that puts under siege the place and privilege of those who once dominated the landscape and controlled the narrative. This in turn sets a high bar to overcome in extending any kind of empathetic welcome or encouraging a sense of shared fate and purpose and, at the same time, underlines the urgency of doing so.

Building a Community of Communities

Yet still, we take as first principles that we must spread that empathy and cannot afford as a country to ignore the diversity in our midst, those whose civic, economic, and cultural participation will better equip us to face down the challenges of our contemporary world. It is very much in our compelling interests, as Patel outlines in his vision of an expanded, more pluralistic, civil religious narrative, to pull together our diverse communities of faith to form a new, more textured unity, one similar to what Danielle Allen referred to in the first volume in this series as a "community of communities." According to her analysis, strong intragroup bonds coexist and even reinforce equally strong intergroup bridges across diverse social identity allegiances.[7] Pragmatic pluralism, to use the term provided by Laurie L. Patton in her commentary, can effectively position America far from either the religious nationalism or the radical secularism likely to splinter groups further. And even as Inazu tempers our optimism here with a call for a modest unity, and Jones's commentary moves the narrative away from the sacred and toward what he calls a civic creedalism, some version of a unifying hymn will surely serve us well.

What will a modest unity look like? What foundation will it be built on, and how can we all encourage it? As all the authors in this volume agree, this modest unity departs first of all from our familiar, normalized Judeo-Christian tradition in that it is not to be easily built on a legacy of assimilation to whiteness and to a sacred melting pot—there is just too much difference now to easily accommodate. Instead, the new pluralism, which they all also believe can and must be accomplished through the hard work of moving from the facts of diversity to lived pluralism,[8] will likely be built on the shared recognition that we really do live in a new world, on several levels.

First, and perhaps most important as a building block of unity, is the recognition by differing doctrinal groups of some similarities in their circumstances of life—the threats, the dreams, the obstacles, and the opportunities desired for their children, for example— even when there are distinct differences in beliefs or practices. Inazu calls this the embrace of *common ground*, even with differences in what is conceived as the *common good*. This recognition that comes from reaching across the religious aisle, so to speak, may well produce more in common than expected, moving us closer to Patel's pluralistic harmony.

Working on common ground is what the civil rights movement of the 1950s and 1960s did so well, as its participants walked hand in hand, and it is what we are seeing in communities across the country today, even as acts of hatred and violence aim to separate. In January 2017, a diverse group of thirty-five leaders from across the political spectrum formed the Latino Jewish Leadership Council to counter the rise of anti-immigrant, anti-Semitic, and xeno-phobic rhetoric. Recently they sharply denounced the events in Charlottesville as confirming "what history teaches us: hate groups start by targeting a specific ethnicity, religion, or community, and then metastasize and end up attacking our broader society."[9] In a similar call to common ground, Jim Winkler, president and general secretary of the National Council of Churches, called on his "evangelical sisters and brothers" to join with his members, some thirty million Christians in more than one hundred thousand local congregations, spanning Orthodox, Anglican, mainline Protestant, and historic peace churches, to renounce the rise of white supremacists and neo-Nazis after Charlottesville.[10]

Such calls for an ecumenical denouncement of hate remind us that the concept of *neighbor* is about more than geographic proximity. It encompasses our moral obligations, our fundamental interdependence, as Newark's famed rabbi Joachim Prinz noted in his speech delivered right before Martin Luther King Jr.'s awe-inspiring call to unity, "I Have a Dream," at the 1963 March on Washington. Rabbi Prinz, by invoking as the core meaning of *neighbor*, "our collective responsibility for the preservation of man's dignity and integrity," implored us all to reach across the aisle to find that worthy soul in others.

As important as such broad and monumental moments of spiritual and moral common ground are, the everyday acts of solidarity matter too, and these should not be forgotten. In February 2017, the *New York Times* reported on a movement among Muslims to raise $130,000 in a short period for the repair of Jewish graves desecrated in Saint Louis and Philadelphia.[11] Meanwhile, in a demonstration of pragmatic pluralism, the Jewish Telegraphic Agency reported recently on how American Muslims are turning to Jews for help in thinking through how to secure their mosques and institutions, working to share lessons learned about the particulars of staying safe in a nervous climate.[12]

When these participants from diverse religious, ethnic, and identity groups come together and pool their knowledge and intelligence in pragmatic problem solving, as occurs now when communities face threats and work on safety, a robust diversity bonus emerges, enabling participants to uncover good solutions and develop a bolstered sense of being in these times together. This kind of broader community building is evident in many faith-based academic institutions too, as when Augsburg University, a Lutheran institution in Minneapolis, joined in common cause to contribute to the education and economic development efforts of its neighbors, a Somali Muslim community.[13] These everyday acts of everyday ethics, as Patton calls them, involving intergroup problem solving, may well be as critical to forging a new modest unity as are the foundational legal and civil protections of freedom of religion that we all importantly count on to secure our place in a pluralistic America.

The everyday work of pluralism certainly occurs in spaces and places explicitly defined by religion and between groups specifically reaching out to build an interfaith geography. It also occurs, importantly, in more routine civil society organizations, as Patel describes. It can be found in our schools, on our sporting fields, and at our museums and hospitals, contexts not explicitly focused on spirituality or affiliated with one or another religious group but rather gathering a broad range of personal traditions together in public. In these shared public civil institutions, while the common purpose is focused elsewhere—on getting a college degree, on mounting an exhibit, on winning a game, on curing a disease—the ground can also be tilled, purposely or by chance, for building the respect, relationships, and commitments to some common good that Patel identifies as best serving our compelling interests. Within the safety of these schools and community centers, there is fertile opportunity for structuring dialogue, as Patel's Interfaith Youth Core, and the intergroup dialogues pioneered by Patricia Gurin and colleagues at the University of Michigan, amply demonstrates.[14] And dialogue, as simple as it sounds and as hard as it is to structure well, goes a long way toward stripping away the blinders of our identity-based stereotypes in order to see others for what they are and see ourselves as we are viewed by others. When, as Patton so persuasively encourages us to do, we listen to the stories of everyday people, adding to the inspiration from larger, heroic myths, something revelatory occurs. For the somewhat unexpected part of forging that pragmatic pluralism in dialogue and storytelling is that it serves to strengthen one's own understanding of self-identity, even as it signals how interdependent we are with other groups and traditions.

The Power of Expressive Symbolism: Uniting and Dividing

As we work to see what is common in our circumstances, the things we fear, and the aspirations we pursue, while still holding firm to our differences, there may come a time when we get better at publicly recounting heroic (and everyday) narratives of more universal struggle and redemption. These expressions in turn can become symbolic, forming a fabric for a civil religion that feels more egalitarian and less about dominance and exclusion. Throughout our history we have tried to do this, sharing universally motivating spirituals like "Amazing Grace" in times of national distress, as President Barack Obama did when he united a nation in grief at the memorial service for those slain in Charleston, centering his themes on grace itself, including the astonishing spiritual reserve of the family members of the shooting victims.[15] Or when elders of a minority Muslim community in Fort Smith, Arkansas, a town that the *New York Times* describes as having a mix of libertarian and Southern Baptist sensibilities, turned out to support a young white man who apologized for his part in the desecration of their mosque.[16] The aftermath of 9/11 brought out similar expressions and gatherings that appealed to our caring national identity, even as the events themselves fed another strain of religious nationalism and exclusionary impulses.

Expressive symbolism has the power to divide or unite, and the future of our pluralism depends in large part on what we publicly embrace. Today, in the face of heated debates about the appropriateness of Confederate monuments in the context of an invigorated white supremacy movement, we hear the surprising, unifying voices of descendants of Jefferson Davis, Robert E. Lee, and Stonewall Jackson, all icons of that brutal, exclusionary past. In interviews in the *New York Times* after Charlottesville, they all agreed in one way or another that these symbols, as personally meaningful to their families as they remain, should not stand where they can associate the contemporary collective public square with a legacy of hate, racism, and religious nationalism.[17] As Derek Black, a former white supremacist and the godson of David Duke, reminds us, a clear line must be drawn between personal ties (he made calls to both family who carried the neo-Nazi torches and friends who counterprotested in Charlottesville) and the public whitewashing of history.[18] And while no good can come of forgetting that history, as we have systematically tried to do in regard to our Native American brethren, we can remember the tragic lessons of the Confederacy and slavery in museums and classrooms, rather than monumentalize them as part of the national civic religion, on which we depend to keep us moving forward, together.

As Patel compels us, let's search for experiences that unify across difference, turning to occasions when our creative expressions and public symbols can reinforce our solidarity. We very much need both the comfort and the inspiration, as we noted at the start of this introduction, of events that transport us, as when the Alvin Ailey Dance Company performs *Revelations* on Mother's Day to a resplendently diverse audience of Muslims, Jews, Christians, atheists, and more. It matters that this happens in one of America's many global cities, with many plural traditions of faith and identity, but it also needs to happen across our country, in places where people may feel disenfranchised by diversity rather than motivated to unite. Let us go everywhere, even with our eyes fully open to the challenges, in pursuit of a "wider sense of we" that may get us through these trying times, as Laurie L. Patton intones.

Out of Many Faiths

1

Religious Diversity and the American Promise

In his book *What It Means to Be an American*, Michael Walzer observes that political theorists since the time of the Greeks have generally assumed that diversity and democracy do not mix well together. A state works best when it is made up of human beings who view themselves, as a consequence of certain bonds of identity, as a single people. Uniformity of belief was understood as especially important for peaceful participatory societies. Walzer summarizes the view of generations of political theorists thus: "One religious communion, it was argued, made one political community."[1]

A few paragraphs later, he writes, "The great exception to this rule is the United States."[2] The American Founders set for themselves the remarkable task of building a religiously diverse democracy, an experiment never before tried at such a scale in human history.

What will it take for the American experiment to thrive in the twenty-first century? That is the question that the Andrew W. Mellon Foundation has set for itself in launching the Our Compelling Interests series. We find ourselves in the midst of what William H. Frey calls, in an essay written for the first volume in the series, "the diversity explosion . . . a demographic force that will remake America."[3] Will the United States leverage the current diversity explosion to promote the common good, or will it blow up in our faces in forms such as open prejudice, rampant discrimination, deeper disunity, further inequality, and identity conflict?

This volume focuses on the topic of religion. The growing immigrant and minority populations in the United States bring different colors, languages, foods, and family patterns, as well as varied expressions of faith. Religion gives individuals a powerful sense of purpose, and it also induces guilt that brings them to the edge of despair. It binds what would otherwise be a random collection of people into a caring community while simultaneously providing a sacred justification for painfully excluding others. Religious language has given the United States some of its most enduring symbols ("city on a hill," "beloved community," "almost chosen people"), and it is the source of a significant amount of the nation's social capital and the inspiration behind many of our most vital civic institutions (universities, hospitals, and social service agencies, for example). This is not an unalloyed good. In a diverse society, symbols, networks, and institutions can just as easily be mobilized in the service of violent conflict as inspiring cooperation.

Of all the various forms of diversity that we speak of these days (race, gender, sexuality, ethnicity, class, and so on), religious diversity may be the one that the Founders came closest to getting right. These (generally) wealthy, (loosely) Christian, (presumably) straight, (most assuredly) white male slaveholders managed to create a constitutional system that protected freedom of religion, barred the federal government from establishing a single church, prevented religious tests for those running for political office, and penned more than a few poetic lines about building a religiously diverse democracy.

Here, for example, is George Washington responding to the Jewish leader Moses Seixas, who wrote the first president a letter asking about the fate of Jews in the new nation: "All possess alike liberty of conscience and immunities of citizenship. It is now no more that toleration is spoken of, as if it was by the indulgence of one class of people that another enjoyed the exercise of their inherent natural rights. For happily the government of the United States, which gives to bigotry no sanction, to persecution no assistance, requires only that they who live under its protection, should demean themselves as good citizens."[4]

James Madison believed that allowing religious diversity to flourish was essential to establishing social peace. In the *Federalist Papers*, he stated, "The degree of security . . . will depend on the number of interests and sects."[5]

Benjamin Franklin appeared to take that counsel to heart when he decided to make a financial contribution to every one of the diverse religious communities building a house of worship in Philadelphia. Just in case there were groups that were not represented, Franklin raised money for a hall in Philadelphia that was, in his words, "expressly for the use of any preacher of any religious persuasion who might desire to say something,"[6] and he explicitly stated that it would be open to Muslim preachers. The religious leaders of Philadelphia expressed their gratitude to Franklin in a variety of ways, including by fulfilling Franklin's wish to celebrate July 4 "arm in arm" and also observing his funeral together.

The Founders intended for the ethic of religious pluralism they were nurturing at home to extend to international relations. President John Adams signed a treaty with Tripoli in 1791 that stated, "As the government of the United States of America is not in any sense founded on the Christian Religion,—as it has in itself no character of enmity against the laws, religion or tranquility of Mussulmen,—and as the said States never have entered into any war or act of hostility against any Mehomitan nation, it is declared by the parties that no pretext arising from religious opinions shall ever produce an interruption of the harmony existing between the countries."[7]

And they were not the first European settlers on the Eastern Seaboard to express such sentiments. Over a century earlier, a group of citizens in present-day Queens, concerned about the threats that Director General Peter Stuyvesant of what was then New Amsterdam (now New York) was leveling against Quakers, gathered to draft a statement of welcome that became known as the Flushing Remonstrance. They wrote, "The law of love, peace and liberty in the states extend[s] to Jews, Turks and Egyptians, as they are considered sonnes of Adam. . . . Our desire is not to offend one of his little ones, in whatsoever form, name or title hee appears in, whether Presbyterian, Independent, Baptist or Quaker, but shall be glad to see anything of God in any of them, desiring to doe unto all men as we desire all men should doe unto us."[8]

And Roger Williams, banished from John Winthrop's Massachusetts Bay Colony for disagreeing with the Puritan insistence on enforcing religious law with civil authority, had this to say about the prospect of a religiously diverse nation in 1644: "And I aske whether or no such as may hold forth other *Worships* or *Religions*, (*Jewes, Turkes,* or *Antichristians*) may not be peaceable and quiet *Subjects,* loving and helpful neighbours, faire and just *dealers,* true and loyall to the *civill government?* It is cleare they may from all *Reason* and *Experience* in many flourishing *Cities* and *Kingdomes* of the World, and so offend not against the civill State and Peace; no incurre the punishment of the *civill* Sword."[9]

It is this long tradition that Barack Obama, the first black president of the United States, recalled during his first inaugural address, standing on the steps of the U.S. Capitol, looking out toward the Lincoln Memorial:

> For we know that our patchwork heritage is a strength, not a weakness. We are a nation of Christians and Muslims, Jews and Hindus, and non-believers. We are shaped by every language and culture, drawn from every end of this Earth; and because we have tasted the bitter swill of civil war and segregation, and emerged from that dark chapter stronger and more united, we cannot help but believe that the old hatreds shall someday pass; that the lines of tribe shall soon dissolve; that as the world grows smaller, our common humanity shall reveal itself; and that America must play its role in ushering a new era of peace.[10]

In many ways the United States has lived out this vision. We are the most religiously devout nation in the West, and the most religiously diverse country in the world, at a time of religious tension, conflict, and crisis. How do we affirm and extend the ethic that welcoming religiously diverse people, nurturing positive relations among them, and facilitating their contributions to the nation is part of the definition of America? Responding to that question is the task of this book.

For my approach, I have chosen to foreground the Muslim situation in America, using it as a window through which to examine broader themes about America and religious diversity. At earlier times in American history, Mormons, Catholics, and Jews would have served as useful vehicles to illustrate the challenges of our religiously diverse democracy. Twenty or forty years from now, Hindus, Buddhists, or atheists may be the most relevant community to focus on. At this moment, the controversies swirling around Muslims are clearly the most salient, and they raise the sharpest questions about America's traditions, values, and identity.

My section is divided into seven chapters. Chapter 1, which you are reading now, lays out some of the key themes and tensions regarding American religious diversity. Chapter 2 tells the story of Cordoba House, more commonly known as the Ground Zero Mosque, using it as an illustration of a Muslim group seeking to serve the nation in a very American way, only to be thwarted by a very un-American religious bigotry. Chapter 3 delves into the anti-Muslim atmosphere of the Trump era, highlighting how the combination of Islamophobic rhetoric, discriminatory policies, and tacit support for anti-Muslim groups has raised even higher barriers to the contributions of Muslims to American society and violated the ethic of religious pluralism. Chapter 4 contextualizes the current anti-Muslim atmosphere within the broader arc of American history, underscoring its similarities to anti-Catholic nativist movements of the past and noting that the positive pluralist response to those nativist movements provided the United States with its self-understanding as a "Judeo-Christian" nation. Chapter 5 asks what it means for a religious community to be or become "American" and explores the manner in which American Muslims are going about this process. Chapter 6 presents a case study of a group called the Inner City Muslim Action Network, which exemplifies, in my mind, America, Islam, and American Islam. Chapter 7 is a short postscript.

The story of Keith Ellison serves as a preview for many of the themes I will discuss in my section. In 2006 Ellison, an African American attorney from Minnesota, became the first Muslim elected to Congress. Glenn Beck, the controversial media personality, had Ellison on his show and marked the historic occasion by saying, "Sir, prove to me that you are not working with our enemies."[11] Representative Virgil Goode of Virginia objected to Ellison's choice to use a Qur'an during his private swearing-in ceremony, writing to his constituents that Ellison's decision was a "wake up" moment for America. The danger was clear: if the nation allowed this to happen, it was a slippery slope to "many more Muslims being elected to office and demanding the use of the Koran." For Goode, the threat was connected to foreigners: "I fear that in the next century we will have many more Muslims in the United States if we do not adopt the strict immigration policies that I believe are necessary to preserve the values and beliefs traditional to the United States of America."[12]

But in the case of Ellison, the description didn't quite fit. Ellison politely pointed out to his fellow congressman that he was the descendant of slaves and that his ancestors had been in this country since 1742. Given that as many as 25 percent of the human beings ripped off the west coast of Africa and brought as slaves to the United States were Muslim, Ellison may well have been "reverting" to his ancestral religion when he converted to Islam in college. In any case, if legitimacy is bestowed by length of ancestry in the homeland, Ellison's is impressive.

The episode, and indeed Ellison himself, casts light on several interesting dynamics, many of which I will discuss over the course of my section. The first and most obvious is that the term *Muslim* is understood to refer to an alien and a threat. In fact, *Muslim* has become something of a multiple-use slur, meaning that it does not necessarily refer to a belief system or religious community but is frequently invoked to signal disgust for any range of minority identities. Don't like the Vietnamese immigrants who own the coffee shop next door, the Mexican laborers doing roof work on your apartment building, the black executive? Call them Muslim. One can almost see the lips of certain people who use it, say, in reference to Barack Obama, curling into a sneer.

On a somewhat different note, Ellison's victory highlighted the internal diversity within the Muslim community in the United States, which is in fact one of its signature qualities. As Su'ad Abdul Khabeer explains in her book *Muslim Cool*, the standard frame on Muslims in America is the "diaspora narrative in which Muslims emigrated from an 'Islamic homeland' to the 'West.'" But while Muslims from at least seventy-seven different countries live in the United States, a 2017 Institute for Social Policy and Understanding report found that approximately half of Muslims were foreign-born and half were native. Moreover, according to the ISPU study, Muslims were the only faith community in the United States with no majority race.[13]

Inevitably, there are tensions between these various communities. Given the volatility of the Muslim world, it stands to reason that diaspora communities carry some vestige of the prejudices, rivalries, and animosities they grew up with, whether it is Salafi versus Sufi, Sunni versus Shia, Pakistani versus Indian, or Asian versus Arab. This is illustrated by the mosques established by first-generation immigrants—this one for Bosnians, that one for Syrians, and so on.

What often draws these various communities together is a shared immigrant identity, but the binding tie of that solidarity often widens the divide between it and another Muslim social experience, that of the African American community. The tension between immigrant identity and African American identity is intensified by a stark class difference, with African American Muslims reporting significantly lower incomes than Arab American, Asian American, and white American Muslims.[14]

In addition to highlighting the interesting ethnic and racial diversity within the Muslim community, Ellison's election underscored "authenticity" tensions as well. While his conversion experience in college took place within a largely African American Muslim context, Ellison is not principally a product of mosques or other Muslim institutions, and he was a relatively unknown quantity in those spaces before the controversy surrounding his election. In fact, Ellison writes in his memoir that he views religion as a private matter and that he's relatively flexible when it comes to religious practice: "If I were Jewish, I would probably be a reform Jew. If I were Christian, I would be one of those come-as-you-are nondenominational Christians. . . . I don't believe in following a strict set of rules to prove my love for God or to prove my faith."[15] Ellison is a vocal proponent of gay marriage and other LGBT rights, and while he has done a great deal to raise awareness of the plight of the Palestinians in Congress, he has also visited Israel and written about the importance of security for the Jewish state.[16]

Both these positions and his relaxed approach to Muslim ritual practice put Ellison at odds with the people who built Muslim institutions like mosques, schools, and advocacy organizations. In fact, for years, the speeches that the leaders of those institutions gave emphasized the importance of strict religious observance, fidelity to the Palestinian cause, and social conservatism. These were the three pillars of Muslim identity, especially in immigrant Muslim communities. Ellison's election put the leaders of these groups in something of a bind. Were they really going to eschew the first Muslim elected to Congress, especially after he was the recipient of ugly Islamophobic attacks, because he didn't toe the line that they drew in the sermons they gave in their mosques? At the same time, by welcoming him onto center stage in their spaces, were they implicitly erasing that line, and with it both their definition of what it meant to be Muslim *and* their authority to be the ones doing the defining?

In this way, the tensions and conversations taking place within the Muslim community in America mirror some of the tensions and conversations taking place within the wider national community. Just as America has to deal with legacies of discrimination against a variety of minority groups, so does Islam have its own marginalized minorities who are now demanding recognition. Just as America is struggling to deal with its internal ethnic and racial diversity, so are Muslims. Just as ethnic and racial differences in America are linked with class differences, so it is with Muslims. Just as there is a fraught authenticity dialogue taking place within America, so American Muslims are negotiating their own authenticity tensions. Just as high-profile terror attacks by Muslims and Islamophobic discrimination against Muslims have complicated the "who is a real American" dialogue across America, so has it complicated the "who is a real Muslim" dialogue within American Islam. And matters are made all the more interesting by the fact that, until quite recently, a common way for immigrant Muslims to prove their Islamic authenticity was to distance themselves from American cultural patterns. These Muslims now find themselves in a moment in which some of their fellow Americans think that exhibiting open prejudice toward Muslims is a way of displaying patriotism.

Ellison's election was also a reminder of the core values of America when it comes to welcoming religious diversity. He of course did take his private oath of office on the Qur'an, and a famous one at that—the translation owned by Thomas Jefferson. In a delicious irony, the congressional district that Virgil Goode represented happened to include Jefferson's Monticello estate. It was near that site that Jefferson, in 1776, had scribbled down this quote from the English philosopher John Locke: "Neither Pagan nor Mahamedan nor Jew ought to be excluded from the civil rights of the Commonwealth because of his religion." And it was not far from where Jefferson, building on Locke, had drafted the Virginia Statute for Religious Freedom, which became the template for subsequent religious freedom laws in the United States, most notably those contained in the First Amendment.[17]

It is interesting to note that this is not the first time that Muslims have played a role in debates about what it means to be an American. As Denise Spellberg writes in her masterful *Thomas Jefferson's Qur'an*, "As they set about creating a new government in the United States, the American Founders, Protestants all, frequently referred to the adherents of Islam as they contemplated the proper scope of religious freedom and individual rights among the nation's present and potential inhabitants. . . . [They] chose Muslims as the test case for the demarcation of the theoretical boundaries of their toleration for *all* believers."[18]

And so, this section may be viewed as one part of a conversation on foundational themes that has taken place across the ages.

Religious Diversity as a Compelling Interest

Previous volumes in this series make a powerful connection between diversity issues and certain forms of inequality. Earl Lewis and Nancy Cantor, in their opening essay for the introductory volume, write, "The structural lines that simultaneously define diversity and solidify inequality along familiar divides—of race, ethnicity, class, home, or birthplace—have in some real way intensified since the civil rights legislation of the 1960's."[19] Thomas Sugrue writes about "the entanglement of growing diversity and entrenched inequality,"[20] showing that the persistent gaps in educational attainment and economic stability between whites on the one side and blacks and Latinos on the other constitute a major problem.

But it is not, at least at the macro level, the principal problem faced by religious minorities in the United States, including Muslims.

A large-scale study by the Pew Research Center in 2007 found that a significant percentage of Muslims were comfortably middle class.[21] CNN reported that Muslims have the second-highest level of educational attainment among major religious communities in the United States.[22] The Pew Research Center found that religious minorities of varying stripes—Hindus, Jews, Buddhists, and Muslims—all have higher levels of four-year college completion than the average American.[23]

There is, of course, no shortage of examples at the personal or local level of prejudice having a deleterious impact on a Muslim family's business or a Muslim student's experience in school. And there are stark differences regarding educational and economic attainment within the Muslim community, but these appear to be tied more to racial identity than to religious identity. All in all, the macro-level data on economic and educational achievement suggest that this is not the most compelling reason why we ought to be interested in engaging religious diversity.

The problems currently facing Muslims take other forms— racist rhetoric that frames Muslims as threats, bigoted civil society movements attempting to block the establishment of Muslim institutions, and discriminatory treatment in immigration policy. These are just some of the barriers Muslims face that hamper their full civic and political participation in American society.

How does differential treatment of religious minorities impact our nation's compelling interests? It is, in the first place, a violation of America's founding ideals. Here is George Washington in 1783, writing to a group of largely Catholic recent arrivals from Ireland: "The bosom of America is open to receive not only the Opulent and respectable Stranger, but the oppressed and persecuted of all Nations And Religions; whom we shall wellcome to a participation of all our rights and previleges, if by decency and propriety of conduct they appear to merit the enjoyment."[24] Such ideals get enshrined in laws requiring equal treatment of all people.

And why is keeping faith with this ideal, and affirming and extending the laws and policies that protect it, a compelling interest? Because a democracy requires the contributions of its citizens. Unlike in a totalitarian system, where all activity is directed by the state, in a democracy it is ordinary citizens who start businesses, practice medicine, teach school, direct plays, coach baseball, write novels, and give blood. "The health of a democratic society may be measured by the quality of functions performed by private citizens," wrote Alexis de Tocqueville in *Democracy in America*.[25] Prejudice and discrimination are not only violations of the identities of directly affected groups; they also hurt society as a whole by acting as an impediment to those groups' participation on these various fronts. Simply put, people who feel excluded are less likely to want, or be able, to contribute.

One of the great strengths of the United States is its rich and thriving civic life. Tocqueville marveled at how associations created by citizens addressed matters ranging from "very general to very particular, immense and small." He dubbed this "the art of association" and referred to it as "the mother science" of America. Why were Americans uniquely good at building civic life? Tocqueville believed it was at least partly due to the distinctive religiosity of the citizenry. He went so far as to call religion the "first" of America's "political institutions," the sites at which Americans learned the "habits of the heart" of democracy.[26]

In his books *Bowling Alone* and *American Grace* (written with David Campbell), Robert Putnam illustrates the crucial role that religion plays in civic life with mountains of empirical evidence. Following Tocqueville, Putnam writes in *Bowling Alone*, "Faith communities in which people worship together are arguably the single most important repository of social capital in America. . . . Churches provide an important incubator for civic skills, civic norms, community interests and civic recruitment."[27] When all is said and done, approximately half of American civil society is somehow related to religious communities, in everything from volunteering to philanthropic giving to membership in community organizations.

American Grace continues this thread, concluding, "Any way you slice it, religious people are simply more generous."[28] That generosity is linked to the social networks that religious communities create, is consistent across diverse theologies, and is channeled toward both parochial religious causes and broader civic involvement. Putnam and Campbell found that people who regularly attend a house of worship are more than twice as likely to volunteer for secular causes than those who do not.

If American democracy depends on the vibrancy of our civic life, and if our civic life depends at least in part on the contributions of religious communities, then it would seem self-evident that facilitating such participation is a compelling interest for American democracy. This should behoove us to commit to the following:

- Guard against religious preference and establishment and continue the American ideal of free exercise for all faith communities.
- Develop a national narrative that is inclusive of our new social reality of high levels of religious diversity.
- Reduce prejudice and openly welcome the myriad contributions of multiple communities (civic, professional, cultural, and so on).
- Facilitate positive relations between diverse religious communities, guarding against conflict and strengthening social cohesion.
- Encourage particular religious communities to harmonize their distinctive traditions with national ideals such as civic participation and pluralism.

Each of these points will be expanded on in the chapters that follow.

What Makes Religious Diversity
Distinct—and Difficult

Just because it is in our compelling interests to build a healthy religiously diverse democracy does not mean it is easy. Democracy
allows us to bring our personal convictions into the public square;
diversity includes both the differences we like and those we don't;
and religion is about, per Paul Tillich, ultimate concerns. It is no
wonder, then, that political theorists across the ages warned against
such a society. In this section, I'd like to highlight the various challenges religious diversity presents to a democracy.

The first challenge is the one posed by the very nature of a religious tradition, at least in the view of John Rawls, who was among
the most prominent philosophers of the twentieth century. Rawls
viewed religious traditions as "comprehensive doctrines" that might
divide the loyalties of religious citizens. How can we be sure that a
Catholic American would give her loyalty to the arrangements
underlying American democracy (free and fair elections, nonestab-
lishment of religion, and so forth) rather than the arrangements
promulgated by, say, the Vatican? More concretely, how do we know
that she will be loyal to the American president over the pope?
Rawls was also concerned that particular religious groups, if they
achieved majority status and attained enough political power, could
seek to impose their comprehensive doctrine. Finally, he was concerned about people, especially elected leaders and government
officials, offering religious reasons as the justification for public
policy. The first principles that form the rationale for public policy,
according to Rawls, ought to be shared by the entire population
rather than the select few who happen to belong to a religious
group. Rawls's famous solution for this challenge was the concept
of "public reason." Simply put, it is the idea that citizens and officials ought to offer reasons whose core values are generally shared
by the whole population rather than just those who subscribe to a
particular religion.[29]

The second key challenge relating to religious diversity is the challenge of the fundamental differences between various religions. The religious studies scholar Stephen Prothero has written compellingly about this challenge. In his book *God Is Not One*, he calls the idea that religions are mostly alike and all paths up the same mountain "pretend pluralism," a notion that might make us feel good on the surface but at its core is "dangerous, disrespectful and untrue."[30] Not only do religions differ in areas like doctrines, rituals, and law, but the expression of one can sometimes be an insult to, or violation of, another. How are non-Jews supposed to view the idea that Jews are God's chosen people, non-Christians meant to countenance the concept that you must hold to the Christian belief that Jesus is Lord and Savior in order to go to heaven, or non-Muslims to reckon with the idea that Muslims have the final revelation and others are incomplete or corrupted? Moreover, the practices of some communities come into direct conflict with others. Muslims typically slaughter and eat cows, goats, or lambs on their holiest of holy days, Eid al Adha, a sacred rite that commemorates God's placing a ram in Ishmael's stead when Abraham goes to sacrifice his son. However, many Hindus, Buddhists, and Jains believe that killing animals for food is forbidden by their religion. Thus, what a Muslim does to fulfill a religious obligation is viewed by hundreds of millions of other believers to be blasphemous. Allowing communities that have fundamentally opposing views on these and other matters of ultimate concern to create social capital, build civic institutions, and express their identities through potent and what some would call tribal symbols is a recipe for religious violence.

A single glance at an international newspaper will show that conflict between different religious communities is all too real, making it a third hazard of religious diversity. Sometimes this conflict takes the form of a civil war between religious communities within the same nation; sometimes it is a religiously fueled conflict between countries. More recently, it has taken the form of high-profile acts of terrorism. This is, of course, one of the principal frames

in which Muslims are presented. (In the pages that follow, I will illustrate that violent Muslim extremism is far less of a danger in the
United States than we have been led to believe by both media stories and the rhetoric of President Donald Trump.)

While religious diversity has not taken an ugly turn into fre-
quent violence in the United States, growing diversity has been shown
to threaten an American treasure: strong communities. Robert
Putnam, whom I quoted earlier on the importance of religion in
animating civic life, also published a landmark study of the relationship between ethnic diversity and social capital called "*E Pluribus
Unum.*" His findings are sobering: "People living in ethnically diverse settings appear to 'hunker down'—that is, to pull in like a tur-
tle." As diversity increases, the qualities that typically characterize a
strong community decrease. The higher the diversity, the more
people distrust their neighbors and the less they volunteer and give
to charity.[31]

Finally, there is the challenge that diversity poses to the continuity of religious identity. This is obviously important to individual
communities, perhaps especially so to religious communities, for
whom specific ways of believing, behaving, and belonging are tied
to ultimate concerns. It also matters to a society seeking pluralism.
Put simply, without strong individual threads, there is no fabric of
pluralism. This is easier to observe than address, precisely because
religious diversity poses a powerful challenge to particular communities. In his study of the identity of Christian adolescents in
the United States, the sociologist Christian Smith observed that
their content knowledge of Christianity approached zero. These
"churched" teenagers were articulate on pop culture, friendships,
college, and sex, but they essentially knew nothing about Jesus, the
cross, or the Bible. Smith claimed it would be more accurate to call
them "moralistic therapeutic deists" than Christians (they believed
in God and believed God wanted them to be good, and that belief
made them feel good). In a section of his book *Soul Searching* titled
"Concluding Unscientific Postscript," Smith surmises that this lack

of content knowledge about Christianity arises from the fact that young Christians live much of their lives in highly religiously diverse environments, communities that do not normally use, share, or affirm the Christian language that these young people are taught in their brief hour or two at church every week.[32] As such, they do not get much practice using this language, and they likely view it as irrelevant to their "school lives," perhaps even counterproductive.

This conclusion would not surprise the scholar Peter Berger. In his book *The Heretical Imperative*, Berger made a simple observation that had a profound influence on social theory: "Modernity pluralizes."[33] Most human beings throughout most of human history, Berger pointed out, had lived within physical, sociological, or psychological bubbles. This enveloping homogeneity had served as a "plausibility structure,"[34] allowing for only a small number of possible identities and creating an environment where these identities were continually strengthened and affirmed.

The obvious negative benefits for those who did not "fit in" notwithstanding, this world had significant benefits for religious communities who viewed the maintenance of particular modes of being, believing, and belonging as moral, righteous, and connected to salvation. In the premodern era, according to Berger, such communities could be reasonably sure that their tradition would persist, that their children would remain within the fold. There were just not that many other viable possibilities present.

According to Berger, modernity changed all of that. Through the melting of physical, sociological, and psychological boundaries, identity moved from, in Berger's famous phrase, "fate to choice."[35] Surrounded by a variety of ways of being, believing, and belonging, individuals born into, say, conservative Catholic families were now fully aware that not everyone said Hail Marys, went to church on Sunday, or refrained from meat during Lent. Other identities were possible.

This introduced a significant challenge to faith groups. Their "taken for granted"[36] status, again in Berger's formulation, had been lost. They were now "voluntary communities."[37] In addition to competing for the attention of their children (something many found frustrating, especially when the stakes included salvation), they had to figure out how to relate to these other identity communities, the very ones that were drawing the attention of their children away.

The Nation and Its Religious Communities

Harvard scholar Diana Eck makes a useful distinction between diversity and pluralism.[38] *Diversity*, she emphasizes, is simply the fact of people with different identities, backgrounds, and worldviews living in close quarters. The term, as she uses it, suggests nothing about how these individuals and communities relate to one another. *Pluralism*, in Eck's definition, is the energetic engagement of difference toward positive ends. Diversity, in other words, is simply a demographic fact; pluralism is a hard-won achievement. That is the goal that the United States has set for itself. Our motto, after all, is *E pluribus unum*—"Out of many, one." In the words of Michael Walzer, the challeng is, "How are we, in the United States, to embrace differences and maintain a common life?"[39]

I define *pluralism* as an ethic that has three main parts: respect for different identities, relationships between diverse communities, and a commitment to the common good. (For a longer explanation, see my book *Interfaith Leadership: A Primer*.)[40]

This definition dovetails with the framework that Danielle Allen presents in her essay "Toward a Connected Society" in the opening volume of Our Compelling Interests: "The ideal of a connected society contrasts with an idea of integration-through-assimilation by orienting us towards becoming a community of communities. . . . A connected society is one in which people can enjoy the bonds of solidarity and community but are equally engaged in the 'bridging' work of bringing diverse communities into positive relations while also individually forming personally valuable relationships across boundaries of difference."[41]

Our Founders viewed religious pluralism not simply as an abstract ideal but as a practical necessity. George Washington, as general of the Continental army, the first truly national institution, sent a stern chastisement to his commanders when he discovered that they had allowed troops to burn the pope in effigy: "In such Circumstances, to be insulting their Religion, is so monstrous, as not to be suffered or excused; indeed instead of offering the most remote insult, it is our duty to address public thanks to these our Brethren."[42]

Washington was at the time attempting to form an alliance with French Catholics in Canada and was also aware that Catholic soldiers from the state of Maryland were part of the Continental army. To accomplish the common project of defeating the British and winning the Revolutionary War, Washington knew he needed troops from different religious communities in the Continental army to respect each other's identities and develop relationships across their differences. In some ways, he bet the American project on it.

It may be useful to consider for a moment the dystopian possibility. Imagine the *unhealthy* religiously diverse democracy, one that does not respect diverse identities, nurture positive relations between various identity communities, or welcome myriad contributions to the common good. Envision the civic infrastructure built by Catholics (all those schools, colleges, hospitals, and social service agencies) blocked by anti-Catholic prejudice. Imagine if the conflict that defined relations between Protestants and Catholics in Belfast or Serbian Christians and Bosnian Muslims in Sarajevo were carried on by diaspora groups in Boston or Chicago. Consider the Khalistan movement, which sought a separate state for Sikhs in the Punjab; involved the murder of an Indian prime minister, Indira Gandhi; and energized diaspora Sikhs all over the world. What if such a movement were to gather steam in the United States?

These examples are, of course, not so farfetched. All of them, in some shape or form, have in fact occurred in the United States and, at some level, still do. It was not so long ago that a virulently anti-Catholic movement sought to block the establishment of Catholic institutions, or that Catholics and Protestants battled each other in the streets of New York City, or that black Muslims in the 1960s talked about a separate state.

This is why a friend of mine likes to say that dealing with diversity is not rocket science; it's harder. Whether we call it achieving pluralism or building the connected society, in this precarious moment we need to do hard work in three key realms: law and policy, civil society (which I use broadly to encompass everything from the arts to protest to religious communities), and civil religion.

In the United States, it is a signature part of our constitutional system that people from different religious communities receive equal treatment under the law and in government policy. We see this in Washington's promise, quoted earlier, that "all possess alike liberty of conscience and immunities of citizenship." It is enshrined in the Virginia Declaration of Religious Freedom, drafted by Thomas Jefferson: "The proscribing any citizen as unworthy of the public confidence by laying upon him an incapacity of being called to offices of trust and emolument, unless he profess or renounce this or that religious opinion, is depriving him injuriously of those privileges and advantages to which in common with his fellow-citizens he has a natural right. . . . All men shall be free to profess, and by argument to maintain, their opinion in matters of religion, and that the same shall in no wise diminish or enlarge their civil capacities."[43] It is under threat today.

With regard to civil society, Putnam and Campbell in *American Grace* note that religiously diverse democracies are prone to violence precisely because religious symbols are so potent, religious networks so large, and religious institutions so strong that when some kind of tension between different religious groups emerges, the conflict can be especially ugly.[44] We see relatively little of that in the United States today. "How can America be both diverse and devout without fracturing along religious lines?"[45] Putnam and Campbell wondered. The reason, they discovered, is that American civil society as it is currently constituted naturally facilitates meaningful relationships between people from different religious communities. Teachers from different religions work together in the same schools, doctors of different faiths cooperate with each other to save lives in American hospitals, and kids who love sports play ball with each other despite doctrinal disagreements that they or their parents might have. In fact, America excels at forming what the sociologist Ashutosh Varshney calls interfaith "networks of engagement,"[46] civic organizations that include people of different faith backgrounds that can keep the peace if and when tensions do flare. As we will see later, such organized interfaith efforts played a crucial role in mid-twentieth-century American history, and they may be poised to do so again.

Finally, there is the complex subject of civil religion. Philip Gorski writes about it compellingly in his recent book, *American Covenant*. "To be part of a tradition," he states, "is to know certain stories, read certain books, admire certain people, and care about certain things. It is to knowingly enter into an ongoing conversation, a conversation that precedes one's birth and continues on after one's death."[47]

The civil religious tradition was first invoked with reference to the United States by the sociologist Robert Bellah in 1967. Bellah spoke of it as the "religious dimension" of the "political realm" and the "founding myth"[48] of our national community. It stands separate from people's traditional faiths but draws freely from religious language to sacralize national symbols. "Imagine Lincoln's or King's or Obama's speeches shorn of all religious references," Gorski says. "Civic poetry would be transformed into political doggerel."[49]

One crucial role that civil religion plays is to hold a diverse society together, to provide us with a narrative that allows people from a range of backgrounds to not only feel American but also feel that there is something sacred in that. As Justice Felix Frankfurter states, "The ultimate foundation of a free society is the binding tie of cohesive sentiment. Such a sentiment is fostered by all those agencies of the mind and spirit which may serve to gather up the traditions of a people, transmit them from generation to generation, and thereby create the continuity of a treasured common life which constitutes a civilization. We live by symbols."[50]

This is a participatory and dynamic process. It is not as if the narrative exists in heaven somewhere and drops bridges of cooperation into diverse neighborhoods and schools. Rather, changes occur on the ground—in demographics, in attitudes, in events—and we discover that our civil religion narrative no longer connects our past with our present and with our hoped-for future in a satisfactory way. So we listen to new voices, we add some symbols and deemphasize others, elevate these stories and demote those, and reinterpret the whole narrative so that we continue being America, or rather, become a better America.

Let me offer a personal story that illustrates how a national narrative impacts lived reality. When I was in junior high school, my grandmother from India came to live with our family. When she would attend functions at my largely white suburban school, dressed in her Indian clothes and speaking with her Indian accent, I quaked with embarrassment. One of my teachers, Mrs. Pellegrino, must have noticed. She called me to her desk in class one day and told me that my Indian grandmother reminded her of her Italian grandmother. She continued, "Outside of native peoples, we all come from somewhere, and we should take pride in our heritage and the customs of our family. Remember what the Statue of Liberty stands for: we are a nation of immigrants." She smiled and told me to get back to my math worksheet. I walked back to my seat feeling more fully American.

Later, in college, when I read the Walter Lippmann line "The way in which the world is imagined determines at any particular moment what men will do," I thought about that experience with Mrs. Pellegrino.[51] Her statement that my grandmother reminded her of her grandmother, and her invocation of the civil religion symbol of the Statue of Liberty and the civil religion narrative that frames the United States as a "nation of immigrants," helped me view myself as part of the American story. In some deep way, it guides what I do today, including what I write here. Alasdair MacIntyre said, "I can only answer the question, 'What am I to do?' if I can answer the prior question 'Of what story or stories do I find myself a part?'"[52] I am an American. I seek to participate in this nation's progress, carve a place in its promise, play a role in its possibility, and add a chapter to its story.

One final note on this subject. Gorski claims that the religious dimensions of American civil religion are drawn from the Judeo-Christian tradition, specifically the Old and New Testaments. While I am grateful to Gorski for his clear writing on the importance of civil religion, I must disagree with his limiting of our civil religion tradition to symbols and vocabularies drawn from two religions. This is especially the case given the fact that the very term *Judeo-Christian* is a civic invention of the 1930s whose purpose was to expand the national community to include the numbers of Jews and Catholics. The phrase has become so woven into our civil religion that people regularly project it back to the beginning of the nation. I offer the details of this story in the pages to come. For right now, the key question is, If religious language and symbols play a significant role in American civil religion, and if America is getting more religiously diverse, then how will other religious vocabularies and experiences be incorporated into our evolving civil religion?

In my section, I explore this challenge specifically in reference to Muslims and Islam. But, as mentioned earlier, Muslims are not the only community raising questions about the nature of belonging in the American nation. In some ways, the growing ranks of those checking "none" on surveys of religious affiliation (approximately 25 percent of the American population as I write, and an even higher percentage of younger Americans) present a more complicated set of issues. They, by definition, do not have a religious vocabulary, at least not in easily recognizable ways that derive from a belief in sacred texts or cosmically inspired figures. While my own section does not deal with these issues, I am glad that the essays by Robert P. Jones and John Inazu in this volume do.

Religious Communities and Their Nation

What does American democracy require of religious communities and their members? As George Washington wrote in his letter to Catholics, "All those who conduct themselves as worthy members of the community are equally entitled to the protection of civil government." What does it mean to be a worthy member of the national community? I believe it is in the compelling interests of both particular religious groups and the broader nation for communities to harmonize their tradition with the highest ideals of the country. How else are we to achieve Washington's dream "to see America among the foremost nations in examples of justice and liberality" unless all communities do their part? Democracy is not a spectator sport.[53]

By *harmonize* I do not mean repeat or duplicate; I mean contribute in a manner that sounds good and improves the song. In *The One and the Many*, Martin E. Marty emphasizes that American civil religion welcomes what he (crediting Johannes Althusius) calls *symbiotes*: new stories, or new interpretations of old stories and central symbols, by minority groups who take care to make their interpretations feel continuous with the core narrative of the larger nation while broadening and extending that narrative.[54]

Martin Luther King Jr. was a master of interpreting old symbols in new ways. "If we are wrong, the Constitution of the United States is wrong," he said in a sermon during the Montgomery bus boycott. A cynic might point out that the Constitution made him only three-fifths of a person, and if he was insisting on his full dignity and equality, he *was* in fact saying the Constitution was wrong. But King was interested less in parsing details than in the poetry and the pragmatics of civil religion. By holding up the Constitution, he was embracing a symbol to which the vast majority of Americans have an emotional bond and with which they associate the core values of liberty and equality. Once that was accomplished, it was a short step to state that the Constitution also accorded *him* liberty and equality.

This is how a diverse society advances and expands. As Marty writes, "You overcome story with story. You break the spell of myth with another myth."[55] Like the invention "Judeo-Christian," you offer a new interpretation that has continuity with the old, you fill it with the awe of sacredness, and sooner or later people not only absorb it but somehow view it as present at the founding.

This is a benefit to the particular community in question. How else will it register its symbols, stories, and interpretations in the national narrative unless it pays attention to that narrative in the first place? It benefits the nation as well, specifically along the lines of the other compelling interests I name. Communities that see themselves as part of American civil religion make contributions, increase our social capital, strengthen our social cohesion, and are far less likely to develop oppositional and separatist identities. Think of this as the inverse of the line quoted by Michael Walzer earlier. If the challenge of the diverse society is to embrace its differences and maintain a common life, the challenge of the particular religious community is to embrace the nation's common life while maintaining its difference.

Lest anyone think that my desire for religious communities to harmonize their identities with America's ideals and traditions is a call for conformity, let me remind you that the American tradition celebrates dissenters of all stripes. Roger Williams and Anne Hutchinson dissented from the theocratic nature of John Winthrop's Massachusetts Bay Colony; Jane Addams dissented from Woodrow Wilson's march into World War I; Woody Guthrie dissented from the gauzy patriotism of Irving Berlin's "God Bless America" by writing "This Land Is Your Land"; and Dorothy Day dissented from just

about every civil authority who crossed her path. All of these figures are part of American civil religion. We name our buildings and
highways after them, read their writings, tell their stories, and sing
their songs. That is a remarkable thing. In American civil religion we
do not deify a position so much as we sacralize a discourse, including the inevitable tensions, as long as said discourse follows certain
norms and observes basic parameters. As Jeffrey Stout writes,
"[Democracy] takes for granted that reasonable people will differ
in their conceptions of piety, in their grounds for hope, in their ultimate concerns, and in their speculations about salvation. Yet it
holds that people who differ on such matters can still exchange reasons with one another intelligibly, cooperate in crafting political arrangements that promote justice and decency in their relations
with one another, and do both of these things without compromising their integrity."[56] You can live out your faith in harmony with
the American tradition by claiming a faith-based conscientious objector status in your refusal to go to war, as Muhammad Ali did, or
by holding up a copy of the Constitution as you relate the story of
your son perishing in a different war, as Khizr Khan did.[57]

Campuses as Models of Religious Pluralism

In closing, let me say a word about how we move forward. Both
Danielle Allen and Patricia Gurin, in their essays in the first volume
of Our Compelling Interests, emphasize that colleges and universities are key sites for building pluralism.[58] I agree entirely. By relying
on talent at every level of the institution, and recognizing that this
talent (scientific, athletic, literary, and so on) comes in a variety of
racial, ethnic, religious, gender, and sexual preference packages,
colleges have become places that proactively recruit diversity. And
because a college is an intense environment, campuses have had to
figure out how to warmly welcome different identities, nurture positive relations between them, and encourage their commitments to
the common good.

I run an organization called Interfaith Youth Core, which works with higher education to create high-quality, sustainable interfaith programming at every level of a college campus, from the strategic plan to the content of first-year student orientations. We work with over five hundred colleges (I have personally visited over one hundred campuses) and have seen the ethic of religious pluralism in action in dozens of places. At DePaul University in Chicago, for example, different religious groups have their own worship space (demonstrating respect for identity), the University Ministry staff runs interfaith dialogue programs (building relationships across religious communities), and the Center for Service Learning proactively engages them in interfaith service efforts that improve Chicago (contributing to the common good).

This is an excellent illustration of the key point that both Allen and Gurin make in their essays: colleges can create arrangements that engage diversity positively and proactively. Colleges are mini civil societies in which the leaders can require the citizens to do certain things—take that academic course, sit through this training, accept a randomly assigned roommate, and so on.

The arrangements promoted by a college have a profound impact on the broader American society. They help set the civic priorities of other institutions (private companies and K–12 schools, for example), create a knowledge base that is utilized by other civic actors, and nurture a society's future leaders. And because so many colleges in the United States were established by faith communities *and* welcome diversity, they also have an opportunity to model how to retain particularity while achieving pluralism.

On this, allow me to share a personal story.

I am in this country because an institution started by French priests in the Indiana countryside in the 1840s, committed to the faith formation and economic uplift of poor midwestern Catholic boys, somehow saw fit to admit a wayward Ismaili Muslim student from Bombay into its MBA program in the 1970s. That man was my father. During his time in South Bend, he developed a fanatic devotion to Fighting Irish football and a deep appreciation for how faith communities in the United States built institutions that served people beyond their immediate groups. He viewed it as part of the definition of being American. You hold on to who you are by tapping into those parts of your identity that inspire you to serve others.

Notre Dame was the site of one of my earliest explicitly interfaith memories. On Football Saturdays, we would take the Skyway out of Chicago, onto I-80, and into South Bend. We grew up in the world before smartphones, so my dad would keep us occupied for the two-hour drive by telling us we could see the Golden Dome across the open fields if we only looked hard enough. Our first stop when we arrived on campus was always the Grotto, a shrine to the Virgin Mary that attracts visitors from all over the world. My father, never a particularly observant Muslim, would close his eyes and cup his hands and rock back and forth in reverence. Once, when I was ten or eleven and had a little Islamic knowledge in my head and a strong desire to skip the Grotto ritual so that we could head straight into the stadium, I pointed out that praying at a shrine dedicated to a statue of a Christian figure was probably not a very Muslim thing to do. My dad gave me the arched-eyebrows look that I now frequently employ as a parent myself, quoted from the Qur'an that God should be imagined as "Light upon Light," and pointed at the hundreds of candles flickering in the cove. Then he put his hand on my shoulder and said, "You have a choice whenever you encounter something from another tradition, Eboo. You can look for the differences, or you can find the resonances. I advise you to find the resonances."

I shared this tale at the sesquicentennial celebration for Boston College a few years ago, and lo and behold, the president of Notre Dame, Father John Jenkins, was in the audience. "You know who would love to hear that story," he said to me after the panel. "Father Hesburgh. You should come to South Bend and share it with him."

You didn't have to tell me that twice. Father Theodore Hesburgh became president of Notre Dame in 1952 at the ripe old age of thirty-five, served in that role for half a century, and was the figure most responsible for leading what was once a modest midwestern parochial school concerned primarily with the faith formation of young Catholic men to the forefront of global academic institutions, all the while maintaining its Catholic identity.

A few weeks later my friend Gabe and I were making the familiar drive out of Chicago onto the Skyway and I-80, looking across the midwestern landscape for glimpses of the Golden Dome. Father Hesburgh welcomed us into his office and asked to hear the story about my father. He nodded as I told it, telling me that it embodied what he hoped Notre Dame would be—a place where people from around the world could connect more deeply with their own identities and develop powerful relationships with people with other identities, all nurtured by the Catholic identity at the core of Notre Dame.

I commented that this is precisely what seemed to be happening at Notre Dame, noting the growing number of Muslim, Evangelical, and Jewish faculty, staff, and board members at the university. Then I asked a pointed question: Were there people within the Fighting Irish family—old-timers, Holy Cross priests, or other types of "traditionalists"—who were less than happy with the growing diversity of the institution? And what did he tell them when they voiced their concerns?

Hesburgh, well into his nineties at that point, perked up, slapped his palm on the desk, and started speaking of the relationship between the large C in *Catholic*, which he said stood for the particular tradition, and the small c in *catholic*, which he pointed out meant "universal." "We have to understand our Catholic tradition in a way that helps us accomplish our catholic mission, which is to lift up the well-being of all."

The success of Notre Dame, even its very existence, was not inevitable. Lyman Beecher, who led a seminary in nearby Cincinnati, made Catholic institutions the object of his anti-Catholic diatribes, claiming that they were a Trojan horse for popery. A few years before Notre Dame's founding, rioters inspired by Beecher's sermons burned down a Catholic educational institution outside Boston, the Ursuline convent. The Catholic university that had educated my father and given my family its initial footing in America might well have suffered a similar fate at the hands of anti-Catholic forces.

I had come to Notre Dame with my close friend Gabe, a Catholic, and he asked for a blessing as we were leaving. Father Ted nodded, then motioned for me to kneel and close my eyes as well. It was, for my friend, a Catholic ritual of great significance. For me, it was an American sacrament.

2

Cordoba House

In early December 2009, the *New York Times* ran an article on a new project in lower Manhattan called Cordoba House. The plan was ambitious, including a five-hundred-seat performing arts center, a gym, a restaurant, a library, a culinary school, a swimming pool, and a prayer space. Two things made the development especially noteworthy: it was located a few blocks from the site of the World Trade Center, and it was being built by American Muslims.[1]

I knew the project's cofounders, Imam Feisal Abdul Rauf and Daisy Khan, a dynamic husband-and-wife team. As so-called moderate Muslims (sometimes the label was meant as a compliment, sometimes as an insult), we had met several times on the interfaith speaking circuit and developed a friendship. Our primary topic of conversation was the development of an American Muslim identity. While this was something each of us had cared about for many years, the subject was made all the more urgent by the horrors of 9/11. The attacks had created an association in the public imagination between Islam and terrorism, putting enormous pressure on American Muslims to prove their loyalty to the country while remaining true to their faith.

As the war on terror gained steam and a simplistic Islam versus the West dichotomy began to dominate policy circles and public discourse, people like us were doing our best to highlight the shared

33

values between the two civilizations. We believed the principle link between America and Islam was the ethic of pluralism.

While most contemporary Muslim-majority nations had a dismal track record regarding pluralism in comparison to their Western counterparts, many medieval Muslim societies were relatively impressive on this score. Of these, the civilization of Al-Andalus was especially inspiring. The Catholic nun Hroswitha described its capital city, Cordoba, as "the brilliant ornament of the world [that] shone in the west, a noble city . . . wealthy and famous . . . and resplendent in all things, and especially for its seven streams of wisdom and as much for its constant victories." The library of the caliph had four hundred thousand volumes, a thousand times more than the largest library in the Christian-dominated parts of Europe. The catalog of the library alone ran to forty-four volumes. Jews, hounded and hated elsewhere in Europe, thrived here. This was the milieu that gave rise to the great Jewish philosopher Maimonides, where Hebrew poetry was rediscovered and reinvented, and where a Jew rose to be the caliph's foreign minister. While much of Europe was experiencing the Dark Ages, Muslim scholars were producing commentaries on Aristotle, texts that played a key role in sparking the Renaissance in Europe.[2]

In our minds, the connections between medieval Andalusia and contemporary America were everywhere. There were beautiful symbolic resonances; synagogues on New York City's Upper West Side contained architectural allusions to the mosques built in eleventh-century Cordoba. And there were deep substantive similarities. Andalusia had experimented with a partial pluralism, extended limited rights to diverse communities, and allowed some degree of civic and political participation. The American project was about the adoption and advancement of this ethic.

Imam Feisal and Daisy named their project Cordoba House to highlight the bridge of pluralism that connected Islam and America. They liked to speak about how Catholicism and Judaism had become American religions by bursting out of their bunkers, learning from and working with other communities, and building institutions that served the common good of their adopted homeland instead of just the concerns of their own parochial groups. Muslims, they insisted, ought to do the same. We could maintain our distinctive identities while contributing to the civic life of our nation. In fact, becoming a valued part of a diverse nation was a deeply Islamic thing to do.

All of this was running through my mind when I read the *Times* article. "They're actually getting this off the ground," I thought to myself, impressed.

The real-estate developer, a Muslim who prayed at Imam Feisal's mosque, stated the intention of the project: "It's really to provide a place of peace, a place of services and solutions for the community." The *Times* quoted a half dozen other people who supported the effort, from government officials to religious leaders to people who had lost loved ones in the 9/11 attacks. A spokeswoman for the National September 11 Memorial and Museum said, "The idea of a cultural center that strengthens ties between Muslims and people of all faiths and backgrounds is positive." An FBI staffer said of Imam Feisal, "We've had positive interactions with him in the past." A woman whose son was killed on 9/11 called it "a noble effort."

Given that it was going to be near Ground Zero, there were some brief references to the "delicate nature" of the project in the *Times* piece. If anybody could pull this off, the article suggested, it would be Imam Feisal. Not only was he a figure with significant national clout, he led a mosque right in the neighborhood. His own Muslim community had been deeply impacted by the tragedy. The *Times* wasn't the only media outlet that leaned positive on the project. In early 2010, the conservative commentator Dr. Laura hosted Daisy Khan on Fox News and declared her support. It looked like clear sailing.

The closest parallel to Cordoba House was the Jewish Community Center in Manhattan, and Imam Feisal and Daisy reached out to them for advice. Joy Levitt, the executive director, was quoted in the *Times* article as saying, "For the J.C.C. to have partners in the Muslim community who share our vision of pluralism and tolerance would be great." She did give Imam Feisal and Daisy some stern advice: leave enough space for baby strollers.

I wasn't worried about stroller space; I was worried about the swimming pool. "That's going to be trouble," I thought to myself. Imam Feisal had always been viewed as a little too liberal by certain contingents within American Islam. Even the *Times* story mentioned that he had a tendency to be "focused more on cultivating relations with those outside the faith than within it." Imam Feisal's unabashed affection for the United States (he'd written a book called *What's Right with Islam Is What's Right with America*), his work with the FBI on the issue of domestic Muslim extremism, his willingness to be identified as a "moderate Muslim"—all of these things had caused grumbling within some segments of his own community.[3] Many wanted more criticism of U.S. foreign policy and popular culture.

As it turns out, those more traditional Muslims never got a chance to raise questions about the Islamic propriety of gender mixing at the Cordoba House swimming pool.

In May 2010, the right-wing blogger and well-known flame thrower Pamela Geller posted a piece referring to Cordoba House as a "Victory Mosque at Ground Zero."[4] The language was picked up by conservative media outlets and quickly set off an acrimonious debate that dominated news cycles, Facebook feeds, and watercooler conversations through the summer and into the fall of that year. Political candidates from Nevada to North Carolina started making their opposition to "the Ground Zero mosque" a core part of their campaign rhetoric. Mosque projects from the suburbs of San Diego to Staten Island—literally, from sea to shining sea—began facing vociferous opposition. Prominent people from the lieutenant governor of Tennessee to Marty Peretz of the *New Republic* questioned whether Muslims were deserving of First Amendment rights. *Time Magazine* ran a cover story titled "Islamophobia: Does America Have a Muslim Problem?"[5]

Perhaps the most high-profile opponent of Cordoba House was the former Speaker of the House of Representatives and soon-to-be presidential candidate Newt Gingrich. He characterized the attempts to establish Cordoba House as "purely and simply an anti-American act of triumphalism on the part of a radical Islamist" and compared it to placing a "Nazi" sign next to the Holocaust Museum.[6] For Gingrich, the name Cordoba referred not to a Muslim civilization that was on the vanguard of pluralism for its time but to "the capital of Muslim conquerors who symbolized their victory over the Christian Spaniards by transforming a church into the world's third-largest mosque complex." He further claimed, "America is experiencing an Islamist cultural-political offensive designed to undermine and destroy our civilization."[7] Such language was quickly turned into talking points that were repeated in thousands of speeches, blogs, and tweets.

Gingrich raised particular concerns about what he called a "stealth jihad": "Stealth jihadists use political, cultural, societal, religious, intellectual tools; violent jihadists use violence," he stated in a widely publicized speech at the American Enterprise Institute in Washington, DC, in July 2010. "But in fact they're both engaged in jihad," he continued, "and they're both seeking to impose the same end state, which is to replace Western civilization with a radical imposition of Shariah."[8]

Sharia literally means "path to the watering place," but it is more colloquially understood as "Islamic law." While this conjures up images of Taliban brutality, much of what is covered in Sharia are straightforward matters regarding prayer and communal life. Furthermore, like the law of any religious tradition or nation, it is by no means fixed but rather requires interpretation and adaptation for various times and places. Gingrich said little about such nuances, content instead for his statements to provide an aerial attack for what was already an aggressive anti-Sharia ground game. Even before the Cordoba House controversy, a small group of anti-Muslim activists were encouraging state legislatures to pass anti-Sharia legislation, measures that would proactively forbid American judges from consulting Sharia law.

Frank Gaffney was one of the leaders of the anti-Sharia movement. In 2010 Gaffney's think tank, the Center for Security Policy, produced a report entitled *Sharia: The Threat to America*, which stated, "Sharia is a doctrine that imposes the rule of Allah over all aspects of society. More precisely, contrary to the Virginia Statute for Religious Freedom, and in a way absolutely incompatible with it, Sharia asserts that God did not create freewill but tied it to the will of Allah—the condition of human beings is submission to Allah and not freedom."[9]

The statement contains or suggests many of the most common tropes of the anti-Muslim movement: Islam is best understood not as a religion but as a political system bent on domination. While in Judeo-Christian America we cherish freedom, Islam requires submission. No wonder their guys committed 9/11. Could your Muslim neighbors be the next jihadists? Better stop them now.

Comments by Gingrich and other national figures gave the anti-Sharia movement hero status in certain circles. By 2014, this movement had convinced over two dozen states to very publicly deliberate barring any reference to Sharia law in their political or judicial system, even though there was no "pro-Sharia" movement of which to speak.

By far the strongest public advocate for Cordoba House was New York City mayor Michael Bloomberg. Other leaders, ranging from Sarah Palin to President Barack Obama, while granting that Muslims had a constitutional right to build Cordoba House, questioned the wisdom and sensitivity of the decision. In contrast, Bloomberg passionately supported the project in its original plan and location.

His most comprehensive statement on behalf of Cordoba House was given in a speech on August 3, 2010, at Governor's Island. With the Statue of Liberty in the background and a group of diverse religious leaders at his side, Bloomberg opened his speech by stating that New York includes people from over one hundred countries, speaking over two hundred languages, and that virtually every religion in the world has some footing in the city.[10]

He layered these comments about diversity with remarks on freedom, calling New York "the freest city in the world" and stating that it was this combination of diversity and freedom that makes New York "special and different and strong."

He highlighted the symbolism of the site. Governor's Island was the place where the earliest European settlers had first set foot in New Amsterdam in the early seventeenth century, and the Statue of Liberty was a beacon of welcome to a new crop of immigrants arriving in New York Harbor 250 years later. People from a remarkable range of backgrounds and identities have come to New York and America, in part attracted by its freedoms.

Bloomberg delineated several core American freedoms but emphasized, "Of all our precious freedoms, the most important may be the freedom to worship as we wish." He spoke passionately about the state's particular role regarding religious freedom. Not only was Cordoba House private property, in which the state may not interfere except under exceptional circumstances, but the government is bound by the First Amendment of the Constitution to protect religious expression. Moreover, not only does the government have a duty of noninterference regarding religious practice, it has an obligation to exhibit fairness to all religious traditions and communities. "This nation was founded on the principle that the government must never choose between religions or favor one over another."

This combination of freedom and diversity poses challenges, Bloomberg conceded. It means that your neighbor has the right (within limits) to express things you may not like, believe things you think are wrong, and act in ways that you view as sinful. This is to be expected in a society that is both free and diverse, and where the government is constitutionally bound to protect the expressions of a variety of groups.

But for the most part, Bloomberg noted, people from diverse backgrounds engage with one another in a spirit of "mutual respect and tolerance . . . openness and acceptance." Sometimes, people go beyond mere tolerance and engage in everything from intentional acts of interfaith cooperation to sacrificial service across lines of difference. The diverse religious leaders who had gathered with him in defense of Cordoba House were doing so out of the deep convictions of their different faiths. Bloomberg became choked up while talking about the first responders on 9/11 who saved the lives of everyone they could. "In rushing into those burning buildings, not one of them asked, 'What God do you pray to?'"

He was forthright about the history of prejudice that many religious communities faced in earlier eras of American history, including in New York City. In the 1650s, Dutch governor Peter Stuyvesant barred Quaker prayer meetings and turned down a petition by Jews to establish a synagogue in Manhattan. Into the 1700s, the practice of Catholicism was effectively prohibited, and priests were subject to arrest. The first Catholic parish was not established until the late eighteenth century, and it stands only a few steps from the proposed site of Cordoba House.

Bloomberg directly addressed the question of prejudice against Muslims. He pointed out that Muslims also died on 9/11 and that it was profoundly wrong and unfair to suggest that the terrorist attack should taint all Muslims or that they were in any way representative of the teachings of Islam. In fact, Bloomberg went on, "we would be untrue to our values and play into our enemies' hands if we were to treat Muslims differently than anyone else."

While prejudice against minority religious communities is certainly part of the history of New York City and the United States, so is another story: standing up for religious tolerance and pluralism. Bloomberg shared the story of how a group of ordinary citizens in the small hamlet of Flushing, Queens, in response to Governor Stuyvesant's ban on Quaker prayer meetings in the 1650s, drafted a document called the Flushing Remonstrance, which stated that they would welcome Quakers with love and protect their religious expression.

Such movements for acceptance, tolerance, and pluralism have not only secured the rights of various groups to free expression in the United States, they have also paved the way for the important civic and social contributions of these communities. Bloomberg believed this would be true for Cordoba House as well, saying that the project's creators envisioned "reaching beyond their walls and building an interfaith community," thus "add[ing] to the life and vitality of the neighborhood and the entire city."

All of this, Bloomberg suggested, was part and parcel of what made America and New York unique, even exceptional. He pointed out that government interference in religion and favoritism for particular faiths happened in other countries, but it should not happen in the United States. He invoked religious language to make his point: "Our values and our traditions endure, and there is no neighborhood in this city that is off-limits to God's love and mercy."

The stark contrast between the views expressed by Mayor Bloomberg and those held by the likes of Speaker Gingrich illustrates two poles in the debate on the presence of Muslims in the United States. Whereas Gingrich and others spoke of American identity as inherently Judeo-Christian, Bloomberg spoke of American identity as essentially plural. Whereas Gingrich and others were part of a movement that overtly attempted to discriminate against and spread prejudice toward a minority religious group, Bloomberg sought to protect that community. Whereas Gingrich and others wanted government to be a party to their prejudice, Bloomberg insisted that government should refrain from interfering in religion and, if anything, should be sensitive to the needs of minority groups. Whereas Gingrich and others largely ignored constitutional questions, Bloomberg highlighted just how essential freedom of religion is to America's foundational governing document. Whereas Gingrich and others linked all Muslims and the tradition of Islam with the terrorist attacks of 9/11, Bloomberg insisted that the worst actions of a fringe minority could never be viewed as the responsibility of the larger community. Whereas Gingrich and others invoked American history, symbols, and sacredness to advocate barring Muslims from establishing Cordoba House, Bloomberg invoked history, symbols, and sacredness in defense of welcoming Cordoba House. Whereas Gingrich and others believed Muslims and their institutions were a threat to American democracy, Bloomberg insisted that they were a contribution. Whereas Bloomberg connected the prejudice he faced as a Jewish American growing up to his solidarity with the Muslims attempting to build Cordoba House, Gingrich seemed blind to the fact that his wife Callista's Catholic faith (Gingrich had attended Mass with her for a decade and converted in March 2009) was once subject to a form of discrimination that paralleled the very Islamophobia he was peddling.

The Cordoba House tale is part of a chapter of American history that is still being written—namely, how Muslims are going to be integrated into the American experiment. On its own terms, it is an interesting and important story. Moreover, it serves as a sort of miniature in which a group of critical questions and a set of compelling interests related to both American religion and American diversity can be studied.

The questions include the following: Will minority religious communities be able to establish and express themselves freely? Will their various contributions to the common life of the nation be welcomed and accepted? Will movements that seek to spread prejudice and discriminate against such groups gain power and hold sway? Will government remain neutral, go out of its way to protect minority groups, or side with nativist movements that seek to marginalize them? What role will constitutional interpretation play? Will the self-understanding of America as a Judeo-Christian nation shift as other religious communities, and communities of those who are not religious, grow in numbers and influence? If such a shift occurs, how will we know it is happening, and what things (symbols, policies, narratives, and so on) will actually change? In what ways will minority religious communities themselves change as they plant themselves in American soil? Will the groups that are making America increasingly diverse religiously, some of which are at each other's throats elsewhere on the planet, relate positively to one another here in the United States, or will they carry conflicts from elsewhere with them?

America's promise is to guarantee equal rights for all identities. This framework of rights facilitates the contributions of these many communities to this single country. That is America's genius. The idea is simple: people whose nation gives them dignity will build up that society. When we say we are an immigrant nation, we mean more than just that various religious and ethnic groups settled here in America, bringing with them their Hebrew prayers and Hindu chants. We are recognizing the fact that the institutions they built benefited not just their own communities but also the common good of this country. The space between Jewish and American or Christian and American is not a barrier; it's a bridge. Those things that make you a better Catholic or Buddhist or Sikh—generosity, compassion, service—also make you a better American. America gains when its immigrants bring the inspiration of their particular heritage across the ocean to these shores and plant it in this soil. Those seeds have grown into Catholic hospitals, Lutheran colleges, Quaker high schools, Southern Baptist disaster-relief organizations, Jewish philanthropy, and much more. The institutional expression of religious identity is the engine of American civil society.

Cordoba House was squarely in this tradition. The vision was to build a civic institution that, in everything from its architecture to its cuisine, expressed the specific identity of its founding community, to intentionally build relationships with other communities, and to make a concrete contribution to the common good. In other words, it was a Muslim community living out the definition of pluralism, and doing so in a way that was symbolic enough to be registered in American civil religion. I had this dream that Americans might speak of pluralism in association with Cordoba the way they spoke of reason in association with Athens or prophetic religion with Jerusalem.

The fact that it was *my* religious community mattered a great deal. I travel to New York frequently. I loved the idea of dropping by Cordoba House for prayer and a gourmet meal inspired by cuisine from Karachi or Amman, stroll through a lobby informed by Islamic design, and watch people of all backgrounds enjoy an institution that people from my religious community had built. One day I would bring my family through, tell my kids that the site of the 9/11 attack was a few blocks away, and yes, that it was perpetrated by people who called themselves Muslim (in reality, the only descriptor that fits is *terrorist*), and then point all around and say that Islam is defined not by the destruction wrought by misfit deviants who misunderstand its values and misuse its name but by the beauty, grandeur, and spirit of service embodied by the building in which they stand. Institutions nurture identities, and those of us who are Muslim in early twenty-first-century America need places that highlight the mutual enrichment on both sides of the hyphen in "Muslim-American."

3

The Islamophobia Industry in the White House

There were hints that the spasm of anti-Muslim sentiment that engulfed the American public in the summer of 2010 around Cordoba House was a one-time affair.

The political figures most associated with the anti–Cordoba House movement of 2010 fared poorly in the elections of 2012. Representatives Allen West and Chip Cravaack, members in good standing of the so-called anti-Muslim caucus in Congress, were defeated. Newt Gingrich, Michele Bachmann, and Rick Santorum, among the most vocally anti-Muslim Republican presidential candidates in the 2012 race, all lost to the eventual nominee, Mitt Romney, a Mormon who had spoken warmly of American religious diversity, including Muslims.

Many of these political figures were rebuffed by fellow Republicans. When Bachmann accused the widely admired Hillary Clinton aide Huma Abedin of having ties to the Muslim Brotherhood, Senator John McCain said, "When anyone, not least a member of Congress, launches specious and degrading attacks against fellow Americans on the basis of nothing more than fear of who they are and ignorance of what they stand for, it undermines the spirit of our nation, and we all grow poorer because of it."[1] Bachmann's former campaign manager went even further, accusing his erstwhile boss of McCarthyist tactics.

Frank Gaffney, the prominent anti-Shariah activist and a leading member of what author Nathan Lean called "the Islamophobia industry," was not deterred.[2] The January 2015 copy of his Center for Security Policy report claimed that 80 percent of American mosques were "incubators of, at best, subversion and, at worst, violence and should be treated accordingly."[3] Gaffney himself was quoted as saying, "Far from being entitled to the protections of our Constitution under the principle of freedom of religion [Sharia] is actually a seditious assault on our Constitution which we are obliged to prosecute, not protect."[4]

But by 2015 the audience for such statements had shrunk considerably. Gaffney himself had been frozen out of many respectable conservative circles. The *Washington Examiner* canceled his column, the Bradley Foundation cut his funding, and he was temporarily banned by the Conservative Political Action Conference for accusing two of its organizers of being agents of the Muslim Brotherhood.

What Gaffney and other members of the "industry of Islamophobia" needed was a new voice to carry their message into the mainstream. Gaffney sensed an opportunity in a flamboyant real-estate developer and reality television star named Donald Trump, who had managed to make the racist "birther" myth that claimed Barack Obama was not born in the United States a serious political problem for the president.

In May 2015, Trump spoke at the National Action Summit for Gaffney's Center for Security Policy, and he received a backstage briefing from its associates on the dangers posed to the United States by Muslims.[5]

Opportunity, in this case, proved to be a two-way street. A month after meeting with the Center for Security Policy, Trump announced his candidacy for president and began repeating Gaffney's talking points on the campaign trail, scoring vigorous applause in the process. Trump claimed to have watched "thousands and thousands" of Arabs in Jersey City cheer as the World Trade Center came down. He stated that Muslims as a group were "very sick" and that the community knew who the terrorists were but refused to turn them in. He said, "Islam hates us." Trump promised that if he became president, he would consider using the mechanisms of the U.S. government to do everything from closing mosques to opening a Muslim registry to banning Muslim immigrants from entering the United States. He cited the reports of Gaffney's organization, including studies with methodologies so faulty that many media outlets refused to use them, as justifications for these positions.[6]

The industry of Islamophobia had found a messenger that not only would return them to the center of public discourse but also would take them to the heights of political power.

Among the critical questions I raised earlier with regard to America's rapidly growing religious diversity was whether minority faith communities would be able to freely establish and express themselves, or whether prejudice and discrimination would serve as both violations of their dignity and barriers to their contribution. Political figures play an especially important role. They represent (or claim to, at least) the nation and its people. They have the force of the government bureaucracy behind them, the power to propose policy, and an unmatched platform for their voice. Put another way, political figures have the unique ability to impact the three areas I highlighted earlier in my section: national narrative, law and policy, and civil society.

Over the course of his candidacy, Trump consistently used his platform to overemphasize violence caused by extremist Muslims and ignore violence done in the name of other ideologies, notably white nationalism. Such rhetoric continued during the early months of Trump's presidency, but this time it was combined with the appointment of advisers who brought a clear record of anti-Muslim views to influential government positions and the advancement of concrete policy initiatives that adversely impacted American Muslims. Accompanying the anti-Muslim rhetoric and policy has been a rise in what might be called "anti-Muslim (un)civil society" groups and activities. The result was not only a poisonous atmosphere that made it harder for Muslims to make civic contributions but also a climate in which viewing Muslims as threats was understood as a patriotic duty.

The Anti-Muslim Narrative

The sheer quantity of Donald Trump's Islamophobic statements can sometimes obscure the highly strategic manner in which he goes about advancing a narrative that nurtures anti-Muslim sentiments. I speak here of the scholarship of cognitive bias developed by Amos Tversky and Daniel Kahneman, captured in Kahneman's book *Thinking, Fast and Slow*.[7] The book highlights how human beings use mental shortcuts, which Kahneman and Tversky call "heuristics," to come to quick judgments about the people around them. These include

- the representation heuristic, wherein a particular image or stereotype represents an abstract category such as "gays" or "Muslims" in people's minds;
- availability bias, wherein people make judgments based on the ease with which they are able to access the information available;
- priming, wherein our brains are "primed" to identify further examples that are like the initial ones that are given (for example, when they are given the set "red, yellow, and blue," people are likely to think "purple, green, and orange," not "one, two, three");
- confirmation bias, wherein people actively seek information that confirms their existing theories, notions, or stereotypes;

- framing, wherein the manner in which a question is stated or a decision is framed greatly affects the choices people tend to make;
- automatic search for causality, wherein people seek a cause-and-effect explanation, often rendered in an easily digestible story, for a particular phenomenon, even when none exists.

Kahneman's and Tversky's work is viewed as the gold-standard explanation for how human beings form their "mental maps" of the world, and it has had a profound effect on fields ranging from professional sports to economics. In listening to Trump, it is uncanny just how profoundly his statements conform to the framework just described, thereby scientifically manipulating our hardwired cognition to promote fear and prejudice about Muslims.

Take, for example, the manner in which Trump responded to the question of a Muslim woman at his second debate with Hillary Clinton. The woman introduced herself as one of the 3.3 million Muslims living in the United States, pointed to the rise in Islamophobia, and asked how the presidential candidates would "help people like me deal with the consequences of being labeled as a threat to the country after the election is over."

After casually dismissing her concern about Islamophobia, Trump went about working people's cognitive biases in a manner perfectly designed to stoke their fears about Muslims. He spoke in detail about 9/11 and other high-profile attacks, called the perpetrators "radical Islamic terrorists," claimed that other Muslims knew what was going on but did not report it, and said that the reason America was impotent in the face of this danger was because President Obama and Hillary Clinton refused to name the cause, which was "radical Islamic terrorism."[8]

In a few short sentences, and to the face of a nervous woman asking a question about discrimination against her religious community during a televised presidential debate, Trump concretized the stereotype of "terrorist" as the controlling image for Muslims (the representation heuristic) and highlighted a handful of high-profile and easy-to-recall instances that supported this image (availability bias). By doing so, he implicitly encouraged people (priming) to identify additional examples that would further cement their stereotype of Muslims as threats (confirmation bias), stated that "there's always a reason for everything" (seeking causality), and filled in that reason: radical Islamic terror.[9]

By stating that there were many Muslims who "see hatred going on" but don't report it, Trump insinuated that the image of Muslim-as-terrorist is perhaps actually not the extreme exception or a violent perversion of the religion but rather emerges from the broader community and tradition. The causal leap our brains make is pretty simple: Islam inspires Muslims to commit terrorism. The Muslims who are violent are violent because they are commanded to be so by their religion. And since even seemingly normal Muslims are complicit in violent Islamic extremism, *all* Muslims should be feared.

Trump made what Tversky and Kahneman highlight as a classic error of cognitive bias. Upon hearing a question that he did not know the answer to or did not want to answer—What are you going to do about how Islamophobia is affecting Muslims?—he substituted a different question, for which he had ready answers: namely, let me tell you why you should fear Muslims.

Except that for Trump this was not a mistake but rather a highly deliberate move, one he repeated frequently. At campaign rallies, he would tell the story of a woman who kindly took in a sick snake, nursed the animal back to health, and was rewarded by a snakebite. Not all such snakes would bite, Trump suggested, but who here wants to take that chance? Better not to allow snakes into your home, however needy they might seem.[10]

This is, of course, a parable about Muslim immigrants (snakes), especially refugees who are clearly suffering (sick snakes) and are hoping to come to America for a better life. We know from the framing studies done by Tversky and Kahneman that people are far more averse to the risk of loss than they are attracted to the possibility of gain, so by highlighting the infinitesimally small chance of a Muslim refugee turning violent, Trump is advancing a national narrative designed to play on people's cognitive biases in order to cultivate anti-Muslim sentiment. Moreover, he contextualizes this fear of Muslims in the frame of patriotism, thereby encouraging people to view hating and fearing Muslims as a requirement for loving and defending America.

Most importantly, the narrative of Muslims as threats does not actually accord with the facts on the ground. Between September 11, 2001, and February 11, 2017, according to *New York Times* columnist Nicholas Kristof, the number of people killed in terrorist attacks by Muslims in the United States was 123. That computes to fewer than 9 people per year. By contrast, America experienced 230,000 murders during that same time span. Kristof points out that ladders, bathtubs, stairs, lightning, and husbands all kill more Americans than Muslim terrorists do. Kristof cites analysis by the University of North Carolina's Charles Kurzman, who determined that the risk an American faces of being killed by a Muslim terrorist was approximately one in six million. Contrast that with the risk of being killed *for being* Muslim in America: one in one million.[11]

Anti-Muslim Policy

Ten days into his presidency, Donald Trump signed an executive order titled "Protection of the Nation from Foreign Terrorist Entry into the United States." The seven nations designated in the document all had overwhelmingly Muslim populations, prompting critics to refer to the policy as a "Muslim ban." While the Trump administration claimed that the purpose was to prevent violent people from entering the United States and had nothing to do with religion, the president himself had stated on a television show that the United States should give preference to Christian refugees. Furthermore, Trump ally Rudy Giuliani boasted that the president had called him specifically to ask how to shape a policy that would effectively ban Muslim immigrants while not making the religious discrimination explicit.

CNN contributor Fareed Zakaria called the policy "truly mysterious" in light of a study by the conservative-leaning Cato Institute that tallied the number of Americans killed on U.S. soil from 1975 to 2015 by citizens of the seven countries in question. That number being zero, Zakaria concluded that the refugees and foreign nationals affected by the policy were simply "the roadkill of Trump's posturing."[12]

While the Muslim ban has drawn a great deal of attention, and is still being debated in the courts, there are other ways that President Trump has advanced anti-Muslim policies. Writing in the *New York Times*, Farhana Khera and Johnathan J. Smith described how the State Department has quietly implemented what Trump called "extreme vetting" for people from Muslim-majority nations who seek to come to the United States. This policy has taken the pedestrian form of new and cumbersome requirements for visa applications, resulting in greater delays and significant backlogs. That is not as controversial as an official law, and it is unlikely to be the subject of regular television news reports, but it accomplishes much the same goal.[13]

Such subtle shifts in government policy are implemented at the agency level through presidential appointees. When Trump ascended to the presidency, he brought several members of the industry of Islamophobia with him. Some got formal jobs in the government, others remained influential advisers. "Trump Pushes Dark View of Islam to Center of U.S. Policy Making" was how a *New York Times* headline described it.[14] Newt Gingrich, with his statements about a stealth jihad, was one of the finalists for vice president. Franklin Graham, who called Islam "a very evil and wicked religion," was one of the most vocal evangelical leaders to support Trump's candidacy, and he was rewarded by being invited to offer a prayer at Trump's inauguration. The national security adviser Michael Flynn had written a book that stated baldly that the United States is in a war against Islam; tweeted the line, "Fear of Muslims is RATIONAL";[15] and served on the board of ACT for America, which the Southern Poverty Law Center considers the largest anti-Muslim group in America.[16] It actually made news when Flynn's successor, Lieutenant General H. R. McMaster, in his first meeting with the staff of the National Security Council, said that "radical Islamic terrorism" was not useful language because terrorists were "un-Islamic."[17]

One of the effects of appointing Islamophobic advisers to key government positions is that longtime federal officials who had a relational approach to engaging Muslims found themselves frozen out of policy-making decisions and ultimately left government work. One of these individuals was George Selim, a Republican who joined the George W. Bush administration in 2004 to work on countering violent extremism and stayed on through the Obama administration doing similar work. Selim's main approach to countering violent extremism was to build positive partnerships with American Muslims, making clear that both presidents he worked for principally viewed Muslims as contributing citizens while recognizing that there was also an extremism problem that had to be addressed and that Muslims were important partners in that. I have been in well over a dozen meetings with Selim, and his respect for and knowledge about Islam and Muslims is evident. Even if Muslim community leaders did not always agree with all of Selim's policy positions, they generally liked and respected him. After six months of the Trump administration and its anti-Muslim atmosphere, Selim decided he couldn't do his job the way he wanted to and left, telling the *Atlantic*'s Peter Beinart, "There were clearly political appointees in this administration who didn't see the value of community partnerships with American Muslims."[18]

By far the most influential official in the Trump campaign and the first months of the administration was Steve Bannon. In many ways,

Bannon is the through line between Trump's anti-Muslim narrative, the anti-Muslim policies of the administration, and the anti-Muslim civic groups that either grew or emerged during the Trump era.[19]

Because of Bannon's wide influence on the Trump administration's anti-Muslim initiatives, it is useful (if unpleasant) to spend some time on the texture of his worldview and the engine of his power. The conservative writer Christopher Caldwell, editor of the *Weekly Standard* and himself the author of a book warning about the (negative, in his view) influence of Islam in Europe,[20] summarized Bannon's mind-set in a *New York Times* op-ed in this way: "Mr. Bannon does not go into detail about what Judeo-Christian culture is, but he knows one thing it is not: Islam. Like most Americans, he believes that Islamism—the extremist political movement—is a dangerous adversary. More controversially he holds that, since this political movement is generated within the sphere of Islam, the growth of Islam—the religion—is itself a problem with which American authorities should occupy themselves."[21]

Bannon displayed this worldview in his career as a Hollywood filmmaker. One of his film outlines was titled, "Destroying the Great Satan: The Rise of Islamic Facism [*sic*] in America." The opening sequence showed the U.S. Capitol with an Islamic flag fluttering above and chants of "Allahu Akbar" rising from inside the building. The outline for the film stated that the United States was in danger of turning into the "Islamic States of America" and that a Muslim fifth column was being enabled, under the guise of tolerance and multiculturalism, by institutions such as the media, the Jewish community, and the government.[22]

Before joining the Trump campaign, Bannon ran the influential conservative website Breitbart News, which he famously described as the "platform for the alt-right." Simply put, the alt-right is a movement of white nationalists. In one study of 447 self-proclaimed members of the movement, researchers asked participants to mark how "evolved" various ethnic, racial, and religious groups are on a scale where 100 is fully evolved and 0 is an ape. The average score of white people among this group representing the alt-right was 91.8. The average scores of Jews, Mexicans, black people, and Muslims were, respectively, 73, 67.7, 64.7, and 55.4.[23]

Given the foregoing data, it should come as no surprise that Islamophobia was a central narrative at Bannon's Breitbart News and a defining feature of the alt-right movement that it nurtured. Bannon, for example, hosted Gaffney on his radio show some thirty times, he picked up Gaffney's column when the *Washington Times* canceled it, and, after Gaffney was banned from the Conservative Political Action Conference, Bannon put him on prominent panels during Breitbart's parallel conference, "The Uninvited."

The alt-right, with its Islamophobic edge, emerged as a civic movement nurtured by Bannon's Breitbart News. Bannon helped turn it into an electoral bloc that supported Trump's candidacy. That candidacy, and especially Trump's victory, in turn energized the civil society movement of anti-Muslim groups.

Anti-Muslim Civil Society

In August 2017, white nationalists staged a demonstration in the quaint college town of Charlottesville, Virginia. They carried torches reminiscent of those at Klan rallies, surrounded themselves with Nazi symbols, and alternated between chants of "You will not replace us" and "Jew will not replace us." While they did not manage to find an appropriate term to rhyme with "Muslim," there is little doubt about the Islamophobic nature of these groups.

David Duke articulated the purpose of the rally, saying, "We are going to fulfill the promises of Donald Trump. That's what we believed in. That's why we voted for Donald Trump, because he said he's going to take our country back."[24] As the day's ugliness was coming to a close, James Alex Fields, who had demonstrated an obsession with Nazism in high school, rammed a car into a group of people who had come to protest white nationalism, killing one and critically wounding several others.

Instead of taking the opportunity to distance himself from such groups, Trump blamed the violence on "many sides" and claimed that some of those who marched alongside Nazi symbols were "fine people." He further refused to call the ramming of a car into a group of counterprotesters an act of "terrorism."

Leaders of those groups appeared elated at Trump's support. Duke thanked him directly. The series of events prompted *Washington Post* columnist Dana Milbank to call the president's residence "White nationalist house."[25]

A few months earlier, Jeremy Joseph Christian, a convicted felon who had taken part in white nationalist events, boarded the MAX train in Portland, Oregon, and began hurling anti-Muslim slurs at a young woman wearing a Muslim headscarf and her African American friend. Three individuals from very different backgrounds intervened to protect the girls. Christian stabbed all three, killing two. When he was arraigned in court, Christian said, "You call it terrorism. I call it patriotism."[26]

These are not isolated incidents but rather signs of the strengthening of a white nationalist movement that has a particularly anti-Muslim emphasis. Four mosques burned within the course of seven weeks in early 2017.[27] A CNN report highlighted that, on average, nine mosques a month have been the target of attacks during the first year of the Trump administration.[28] A Southern Poverty Law Center report stated that organized anti-Muslim hate groups tripled in 2016, and it explicitly connected this alarming rise to the Trump campaign's "incendiary rhetoric" about Muslims.[29] The report went on to highlight that the number of "in-person" extreme events declined in 2016 because so many radical right-wing white nationalists chose to go to Trump rallies instead of holding their own. "They were so turned on by what was happening in the pro-Trump world that they entered that world, rather than holding their own rallies. . . . Trump has coopted many of the issues of the radical right," said Mark Potok, the author of the report.[30]

Does Trump's anti-Muslim rhetoric play any role in these actions? There is interesting social science that suggests that xenophobic narratives from people in positions of authority create an enabling environment for others to openly display bigoted speech and act in bigoted ways. Maria Konnikova, writing in the *New Yorker*, sums up the research thus: "If someone in a powerful position acts in a certain way or expresses a certain view, we implicitly assume that those actions and views are associated with power, and that emulating them might be to our advantage."[31]

And yet, in his rhetoric, Trump consistently overemphasizes violence committed by Muslims while ignoring violence committed by white nationalists. On June 3, 2017, a group of Muslim extremists used a van as a weapon in the heart of London, killing seven people and injuring nearly fifty others. Trump quickly condemned the attack with his personal Twitter handle, using the moment to justify sweeping anti-Muslim policies (more on those later), criticizing London's mayor (who is a Muslim) for counseling Londoners to remain calm, and claiming that "we must stop being politically correct."[32]

In contrast, when a white nationalist gunman entered a Quebec City mosque on January 29, 2017, and shot six Muslims dead, Trump was silent.[33]

The Trump administration justifies its constant drumbeat of references linking Muslims with violence by claiming that the mainstream media underreports Muslim extremism and thereby creates a sense of complacency about the nature of the threat. Here is the president on the matter during a speech at MacDill Air Force Base in Tampa, Florida: "Radical Islamic terrorists are determined to strike our homeland as they did on 9/11, as they did from Boston to Orlando to San Bernardino. All over Europe it's happening. It's to a point where it's not even being reported and, in many cases, the very, very dishonest press doesn't want to report it."[34]

In connection with this statement, the White House released a list of seventy-eight terrorist attacks that had taken place since

September 2014, declaring that "most have not received the media attention they deserved."[35] The *New York Times* analysis found this to be patently false—nearly all the incidents had received attention. Moreover, the vast majority of the attacks had occurred outside the United States, undermining the Trump administration's assertion that the jihadi threat was something that should keep Americans up at night.[36]

The trial of Dylann Roof had taken place only two months before the Trump administration released its list. Roof had gone to the famous Mother Emanuel church in Charleston, South Carolina, participated in a worship service with its pastor and several of its members, and then gunned nine of them down in cold blood. In preparation for his act of terrorism, Roof had loaded eight clips of hollow-point ammunition into his Glock 45 semiautomatic handgun because he wanted to use eighty-eight bullets, white nationalist code for "Heil Hitler."[37]

There was no mention of Roof's terrorist attack on the Trump administration's list of seventy-eight extremist events.

Another revealing example: Trump adviser Kellyanne Conway, in an effort to highlight the threat posed by Muslim extremists to the American homeland, spoke multiple times of the "Bowling Green massacre."[38]

But extremist Muslims had never plotted an attack in Bowling Green.

As it turns out, Richard Schmidt, a middle-aged white man who owned a sports memorabilia business, had. In 2012, a federal raid uncovered eighteen firearms—including multiple assault rifles— racist writings, and the names and addresses of African American and Jewish leaders that Schmidt was planning to kill. The government came to believe that Schmidt was involved with white supremacist and neo-Nazi groups. "This defendant, quite simply, was a well-funded, well-armed and focused one-man army of racial and religious hate,"[39] said prosecutors in a court filing.

Conway made no mention of Schmidt when she cited the Bowling Green massacre, nor did any other Trump administration officials as they criticized the media for ignoring extremism. Writer A. C. Thompson notes, "For some concerned about America's vulnerability to terrorism, the very real, mostly forgotten case of Richard Schmidt in Bowling Green, Ohio, deserves an important place in any debate of what is real and what is fake, what gets reported on by the news media and what doesn't. Those deeply worried about domestic far-right terrorism believe United States authorities, across many administrations, have regularly underplayed the threat, and that the news media has repeatedly underreported it. Perhaps we have become trapped in one view of what constitutes the terrorist threat, and as the case of Mr. Schmidt shows, that's a problem."[40]

It is interesting to note the intersections between federal policy under Trump and the trap that Thompson writes of. An organization called Life after Hate, which focuses on rehabilitating neo-Nazis and skinheads, was awarded a grant from the Department of Homeland Security to expand its work under President Obama's Homeland Security secretary, Jeh Johnson. When the Trump administration came in, it withdrew the grant without explanation. This also was part of a larger pattern. An analysis by the *New York Times* found that nearly all of the grants that the Trump administration has given out to fight extremism have gone to organizations focused exclusively on combating Islamic terrorism, even though white supremacist groups have been responsible for more homicides since 9/11 than any other extremist movement.[41]

It would be concerning enough if Trump and his allies had somehow unwittingly fallen into the trap of overemphasizing the threat posed by a religious minority while ignoring more familiar types of homegrown extremism. The harsh truth is that they are the company who designed the trap, and their instrument has successfully ensnared much of the nation.

Banning the Muslim Contribution

As I wrote earlier, a democratic society relies on the contributions of its citizens in everything from launching technology companies to joining the PTA. Discrimination against an identity group in a democratic society is not just a violation of their dignity, it is a barrier to their contribution.

The contributions of Muslims to American civilization are impressive and wide ranging, captured well in the speech President Obama gave in Cairo on June 4, 2009: "American Muslims have enriched the United States. They have fought in our wars, served in government, stood for civil rights, started businesses, taught at our Universities, excelled in our sports arenas, won Nobel Prizes, built our tallest building, and lit the Olympic Torch."[42]

The atmosphere of Islamophobia in the Trump era has created special hardships for Muslims, a dynamic that hurts both the Muslim community and the nation to which they seek to contribute. Consider the following examples.

Dr. Amer Al Homssi had left his patients in Chicago for a few days to get married in the United Arab Emirates but was prevented from flying back to the United States because he carried a Syrian passport. When he arrived at Abu Dhabi International Airport at four o'clock in the morning, a security officer drew a black line through his visa, labeling it "canceled." In Chicago, thirty of his physician colleagues showed up at a court hearing to show their support. When he finally returned, Al Homssi went straight from O'Hare Airport to his workplace, the University of Illinois College of Medicine/Advocate Christ Medical Center. "I'm very anxious to get back to my residency, back to my patients, back to my colleagues. I'm very delighted to be here to do my work."[43]

There have been several reports of physicians like Dr. Al Homssi whose lives and contributions were disrupted because of Trump's Muslim ban. The sad irony here is that these physicians often serve in areas that include high concentrations of Trump voters. The Medicus Firm, which recruits physicians for hard-to-fill jobs, reported that, across the United States, there are more than fifteen thousand doctors from the seven Muslim-majority countries covered by the initial travel ban. As the *New York Times* reported, "Foreign-born physicians have become crucial to the delivery of medical care in the United States. They work in small towns where there are no other doctors, in poor urban neighborhoods and in Veterans Affairs hospitals. Forty-two percent of office visits in rural American are with foreign-born physicians, according to the American Academy of Family Physicians."[44]

Muslim immigrants help American small cities and towns in other ways as well. Muslims who emigrated from Turkey have played an important role in rebuilding Dayton, Ohio. With fourteen thousand empty dwellings serving as magnets for drugs and crime, Dayton officials started paying attention to the improvements that the Turkish Muslims were making to neighborhoods in which they had settled, and decided to ask them and other immigrant communities, also largely Muslim, to do more. Mayor Gary Leitzell told the *New York Times* his thought process: "Turkish families could come to Dayton and fix up 4,000 houses. So how do we facilitate their success?" Dayton officials started investing in services that would make immigrants feel welcome, including things that would accommodate their Islamic faith. The civic renewal under way shows that Dayton's efforts are paying off. A Muslim organization called the Islamic Center of Peace recently bought a block-long shopping center that was scheduled for demolition and plans to turn it into a hybrid recreational, commercial, and religious institution. The basic description and the mission make it sound a little like Cordoba House. The president of the Islamic Center said of his project, "I want my community to prove we are part of the community at large."[45]

Based on the positive experience of cities like Dayton, some small-town leaders are doing their best to entice Muslim immigrants to their areas, and they are finding their efforts frustrated by both the rhetoric and policies of the Trump administration. Christopher Louras, the mayor of Rutland, Vermont, believes that refugees from Syria could prove to be a major asset for his town. After his city was officially selected as a refugee resettlement site by the State Department, he commented, "I saw that as an opportunity to grow our population, bring in individuals, families, new Americans from Syria who have a strong work ethic, who were fleeing for their lives and looking to rebuild those shattered lives." Rutland's population is both declining and aging, processes that have dramatically slowed its economic activity. Factories that once made marble are gone, and Rutland, like other small towns in Vermont, has found itself in a fight against heroin. Along with drugs and population decline, Mayor Louras has had to do battle with a civic group called Rutland First that has emerged to oppose his plan for welcoming Syrians and other refugees and immigrants. An online petition against the resettlement plan justified its position by referring to the refugees as "the same people who hate us." The *New York Times* describes the Facebook page of Rutland First as riddled with "vitriolic and obscene comments about refugees." Still, Mayor Louras and his supporters are hopeful. As Lyle Jepson, the executive director of the Rutland Economic Corporation said, "Frankly, we need help. We need people to join our community."[46]

Interfaith Resistance

The careful reader will have noted that thus far I have not used the term *civil religion* to refer to Trump's rhetoric about Muslims, employing the somewhat less potent phrase *national narrative* instead. No doubt American presidents play a significant role in articulating the character of the nation by offering new definitions of its key symbols. It was, after all, John F. Kennedy and Ronald Reagan who virtually resurrected John Winthrop's "city on a hill" metaphor, shifting its definition from Winthrop's narrow Puritan one to the broader one of a nation of diverse people bound by mutual loyalty and equal dignity.

Trump has undoubtedly succeeded in making fear and hatred of Muslims part of our national narrative, at least for the time being. Has he succeeded in making Islamophobia part of our civil religion? He has most certainly associated his worldview with key American symbols—for example, by criticizing professional football players for kneeling during the national anthem. But in America's diverse democracy, the voices and actions of presidents are not the only voices and actions that register. Another resonant characterization of the United States—"the beloved community"—was advanced by an individual who never held elective office and who, in the name of American ideals, opposed many midcentury American laws and held no small number of senior political figures to account. That man, of course, was Martin Luther King Jr.

The Trump era has seen an outpouring of rhetoric and activity that defends the dignity of American Muslims, warmly welcomes their contribution, and advances interfaith cooperation, all in the name of the American ideal of religious pluralism. Members of the legal community, for example, lost little time in challenging the Trump administration's anti-Muslim policies. The acting attorney general of the United States and the attorneys general of the states of Washington and Minnesota pointed to Trump's own anti-Muslim campaign rhetoric in their refusal to comply with the executive order. A federal district court in Virginia agreed with this argument, stating that the president acted with clear animus toward Muslims. The ruling prompted University of Chicago law professor Eric Posner to comment, "This is surely the first time a court has ruled that a president acted out of bigotry."[47]

The administration's revised executive order (covering six of the original seven countries and allowing Muslim green card holders to enter the country) met the same fate. The United States Court of Appeals for the Fourth Circuit, based in Richmond, Virginia, wrote that national security "is not the true reason" for the order and that it "drips with religious intolerance, animus and discrimination." Legal scholar Noah Feldman commented on the ruling thus: "It's extraordinary for a federal court to tell the president that he's lying; I certainly can't think of any other examples in my lifetime."[48]

There has also been a surge in civil society groups opposing Trump's rhetoric and policies and advancing the cause of religious pluralism. Trump's Muslim ban gave people both a concrete policy to protest and an obvious place to do it: airports. Thousands of people from a variety of backgrounds showed up carrying signs saying "Let Them In" and "Welcome to America." A *Chicago Tribune* photographer captured an image of Muslim and Jewish fathers at O'Hare Airport carrying smiling children on their shoulders, one carrying a sign that said "Love" and the other a sign that said "Hate Has No Home Here." The picture quickly went viral and expressed the mood of interfaith solidarity against xenophobia.[49]

Jews were an especially visible presence in these protests. The rising white nationalism during the Trump campaign had expressed itself in a spate of ugly anti-Semitic incidents, ranging from a shocking rise in slurs such as the "Jew will not replace us" chant, to the desecration of Jewish gravestones, to bomb threats at Jewish schools and community centers.

In fact, the dual rising hates of anti-Semitism and Islamophobia during the Trump era have served as a bridge over the troubled waters of Middle Eastern politics for Muslim and Jewish groups. Interest in grassroots organizations such as the Sisterhood of Salaam Shalom exploded, and Muslim-Jewish councils began to be established in cities across the country and on the national level.[50]

In a widely reported speech, Jonathan Greenblatt, the president of the Anti-Defamation League, in response to Trump's threat to create a registry for Muslims, said, "If one day Muslim Americans will be forced to register their identities, then that is the day that this proud Jew will register as a Muslim."[51]

Muslim civic leaders reached out their hands as well. Two prominent activists, Linda Sarsour and Tarek El-Messidi, launched a fund-raising campaign to repair Jewish gravesites desecrated in Saint Louis and Philadelphia. They exceeded their original $20,000 goal many times over, collecting over $130,000. El-Messidi volunteered at the Philadelphia cemetery where the vandalism had occurred, later writing on Facebook, "Seeing this in person was very devastating. Many people there were embracing one another in tears due to what they saw. I want to ask all Muslims to reach out to your Jewish brothers and sisters and stand together against this bigotry."[52]

Colleges have been the sites of some of the most inspiring interfaith activities in response to the Trump rhetoric, as well as the launching pads for interfaith leaders who have played an important role on the national stage. A case in point: not only has Duke's chief representative for Muslim affairs, Imam Abdullah Antepli, organized dialogue trips for Muslim and Jewish leaders to Israel and the Palestinian territories, he also offered the following prayer before the United States Congress on October 4, 2017: "As the Creator of all, you made us different. Enable us to understand, appreciate and celebrate our differences."[53]

Will this activity be enough to form a new civil religion narrative that not only opposes Islamophobia but proactively includes Muslims in the American community? In the next section, we will see how a similar movement accomplished this goal for Jews and Catholics, who were once viewed as foreigners and threats—much as American Muslims are today—but are now warmly welcomed under the civil religion banner of "Judeo-Christian America."

4

Toward an Interfaith America

Nativist Movements

The groups and voices that have emerged to demonize and discriminate against Muslims and raise barriers to their participation in American life can best be described as a nativist movement. American nativism has a long history and often combines a focused anti-immigrant campaign with what Peter Beinart calls efforts to "denationalize" those members of the targeted identity group already living in the homeland, often by associating them with foreign threats.[1]

Among the most consistent targets of nativist movements in the United States have been Catholics. These days, with Catholics serving in the highest levels of American government and a highly visible and widely admired pope, it is hard to imagine just how rampant and focused anti-Catholic sentiment was in the United States for, literally, centuries. Moreover, it is remarkable how much the underlying logic of anti-Catholic arguments shares with anti-Muslim sentiments today.

As with rhetoric about Islam today, anti-Catholic movements of the past claimed Catholicism was a political system that inherently produced totalitarian arrangements that were inimical to democratic life and American ideas of freedom. Hiram Wesley Evans, the imperial wizard of the Ku Klux Klan, which in its early twentieth-century incarnation was a largely anti-Catholic organization boasting three million members, wrote, "We believe that its official position and its dogma, its theocratic autocracy and its claim to full authority in temporal as well as spiritual matters, all make it impossible for it as a church, or for its members if they obey it, to cooperate in a free democracy in which Church and State have been separated."[2]

As has occurred with anti-Muslim movements today, anti-Catholicism reached such a fever pitch that it grew from a civil society movement into a political movement with significant government influence. In 1854, the Know-Nothing Party, whose members pledged to oppose the pope and stare down the Irish Catholics who had grown to appreciable numbers in several American cities, won seventy-five seats in Congress.

As do the movements against Islam and Muslims today, anti-Catholic movements made wild and crazy claims. In 1928, they accused the Democratic candidate for president, Al Smith, who had recently served as governor of the state of New York, of building the Holland Tunnel as a way to smuggle the pope into Manhattan, where he would begin his rule over the United States.[3]

As do members of movements against Islam today, the anti-Catholic forces delighted in selectively quoting scripture and other sacred sources as proof of the faith's nefarious designs. A favorite was this one from the pope in 1895: "Unless by necessity to do otherwise, Catholics ought to prefer to associate with other Catholics."[4]

As do anti-Muslim groups today, anti-Catholic forces resorted to fabrications to make their case. In 1836, a Protestant woman named Maria Monk published her memoirs detailing her experience being held captive in a Montreal monastery, where she was subjected to the predatory sexual fantasies of priests and witness to the buried corpses of the illegitimate children of nuns.[5] Monk's account was one of the best sellers of antebellum culture. It was also a pack of lies.

Monk's book was published right about the time a steady stream of Catholic immigrants from Ireland began appearing on the Atlantic Seaboard. Fintan O'Toole, writing in the *New York Times*, refers to them as "the most destitute national group ever to arrive on American shores. . . . Worse, these people were religious aliens—the papist hordes who threatened to swamp Protestant civilization and, in their ignorance and superstition, destroy enlightened democratic American values."[6] Their arrival was viciously opposed by a nativist movement, and their growing numbers were met with ugly attempts at denationalization and overt, often violent, discrimination. Their descendants include Sean Spicer, Steve Bannon, Frank Gaffney, Kellyanne Conway, and John F. Kelly, people who devised, implemented, or defended policies that specifically targeted American Muslims, policies whose underlying logic was invented by people seeking to keep their own ancestors out.

Judeo-Christian America

In the summer of 2014, Bannon gave a lecture via Skype to a meeting of the Institute for Human Dignity, a conservative Catholic group based in Rome, in which he discussed "the struggle against Islam." He described the current situation as simply a repeat of what the West has faced in the past, stating, "If you look back at the long history of the Judeo-Christian West's struggle against Islam, I believe that our forefathers kept their stance, and I think they did the right thing. I think they kept it [Islam] out of the world, whether it was Vienne or Tours, or other places. . . . It bequeathed to us the great institution that is the church of the West."[7]

It is interesting that Bannon, famous for his interest in history, would speak of the "Judeo-Christian West" as if its creation were a commandment handed down from God to Moses on Mount Sinai and then further enshrined in the Magna Carta and the Declaration of Independence. The reality is that it was largely the invention of a mid-twentieth-century American interfaith organization called the

National Conference of Christian and Jews (NCCJ) that took as its goal the expansion of America's definition of itself.

"[The United States] is a Protestant country, and the Catholics and Jews are here under sufferance." Thus spoke President Franklin Delano Roosevelt, an illustration that the Protestant definition of America was deeply ingrained and would be fiercely protected by everyone from the East Coast patrician in the Oval Office to the midwestern working-class whites who made up the base of the Ku Klux Klan.[8]

The NCCJ and its allies set out to change that. Their strategy was to define the animus toward Jews and Catholics as un-American. This required efforts in the three realms I have emphasized throughout this book: civil society, law and policy, and civil religion.

The success of the movement is most striking, to me at least, in the area of civil religion. That a wide array of Americans use the term *Judeo-Christian* when referring to the United States or the West more broadly is a stunning shift. As straight theology, it is highly suspect. Jesus is, after all, the central figure in Christianity but barely a bit player in Judaism. Moreover, for centuries Christians understood their sacred scripture, which they tellingly call the New Testament, as abrogating much of what is contained in that inferior document, the Old Testament. Unsurprisingly, Jews did not see matters in quite the same way.

Judeo-Christian is on equally shaky ground as straight history, if history is a record of events that actually happened. As the historian Richard Bulliet points out, "European Christians and Jews . . . share a history of cohabitation that was more often tragic than constructive." Jews were (falsely) blamed and (actually) massacred for causing the Black Death in the middle of the fourteenth century; Jews were (falsely) blamed and (actually) massacred for diluting the Aryan bloodline and weakening the German economy in the middle of the twentieth century. A good part of Western history follows this morbid pattern, making Bulliet's line, if anything, an understatement.[9]

As civil religion, however, *Judeo-Christian* is genius. It expands the national narrative in a manner that dignifies previously marginalized occupants, and it makes the process feel not like the civic invention it is but like the rediscovery of a great sacred truth. The NCCJ, therefore, was not advancing a national fiction but rather bringing to earth a lost piece of the Kingdom.

Specifically, they were bringing it to America. The United States was at war with a Europe that had turned to totalitarianism, a social arrangement that grew organically from the evil lie that one race, and one religion, was superior to another. Or so NCCJ officials argued. America would battle this not only with its superior military but also with its superior values. In an entrepreneurial intersection of civil society and national policy, NCCJ trios—made up of a Protestant, a Catholic, and a Jew—visited 778 U.S. military installations during World War II, firing up the troops by telling them they were fighting for the American way of life: "This religious and cultural freedom, so essentially a part of the American tradition and our dream of the Good Society, must be maintained and made secure through mutual understanding, appreciation, cooperation and the elimination of hate, prejudice, and discrimination in human relations."[10]

The palpable irony in all of this, given America's own history of racism and religious prejudice, was not lost on a certain class of civic leaders. Roy Wilkins, a prominent African American activist who would go on to lead the NAACP, remarked, "Hitler jammed our white people into their logically untenable position. Forced to oppose him for the sake of the life of the nation, they were jockeyed into declaring against their own racial theories." And, of course, their religious ones as well.[11]

In the best American pragmatist tradition, many of these leaders spent little energy on highlighting the obvious hypocrisy and instead saw the moment as an opening for them to work to align the reality with the ideal. For example, they seized on the Four Chaplains incident, a naturally dramatic and inspiring story in which two

Protestant pastors, a Catholic priest, and a Jewish rabbi gave up their life jackets to scared soldiers on the sinking USS *Dorchester*, a U.S. naval vessel that had been hit by a torpedo from a German U-boat. After saving the lives of these soldiers, the chaplains then joined arms and jumped to their deaths in the roiling ocean, each with the prayers of his own religion on his lips. Policy makers and interfaith activists quickly recognized the symbolic potency of this event. They wrote articles about the Four Chaplains (forever capitalized out of respect for their heroic deeds), had a postage stamp made in their likeness, encouraged Warner Brothers to turn the story into a film, and built the Chapel of Four Chaplains at Temple University in Philadelphia.

Interfaith activists also worked for changes in law and policy. In 1938, United States Supreme Court justice Harlan Fiske wrote about minorities characterized by "race, religion, and national origin" in the footnote of his decision on *Caroeve Products v. the United States*, stating that the courts would be vigilant in protecting these groups against discriminatory legislation passed by majorities. That same year, New York State revised the Bill of Rights to its constitution. The new version included the following line: "No person shall, because of race, color, creed or religion, be subjected to any discrimination in his civil rights." Such language foreshadowed the civil rights movement.[12]

Slowly but surely, the change was absorbed into the national DNA. By 1955, the sociologist Will Herberg proclaimed that Protestantism, Catholicism, and Judaism were all equally legitimate ways of being American. In 1960, John F. Kennedy, a (not so observant) Catholic, won the White House, embarrassing the anti-Catholic evangelical Protestants who had proclaimed him a stooge of the pope and a national danger. In 1965, Paul VI made the first-ever visit by a pope to the United States. He met with President Lyndon Johnson and did not try to overthrow him. Pope John Paul II made seven trips to the United States and was viewed by many as America's most important moral ally in the fight for freedom and democracy against atheistic communism. There were several years in the 2000s during which the Supreme Court was made up entirely of Catholics and Jews, and a study done by Robert Putnam and David Campbell during that same decade found that Catholics and Jews were among the most-liked religious groups in the country.[13]

Sometime over the course of the preceding events, any one of which would have sufficed as proof of a hostile takeover of American institutions by alien religious forces just a few decades earlier, referring to America as a Judeo-Christian country became as natural as setting off fireworks on July 4.

Beyond *Judeo-Christian*

It is a supreme irony that some of the very people who were dignified as Americans by the civic invention *Judeo-Christian* are now wielding it as a bludgeon to denationalize others. After all, the "great institution that is the church of the West" that Bannon refers to in his Skype lecture for the Institute for Human Dignity was called "the whore of Rome" by the nativist groups who harassed his Irish Catholic ancestors as they sought their footing in the United States. Conservative columnist Dennis Prager proclaimed that Keith Ellison's decision to use the Qur'an instead of the Bible for his swearing-in should be opposed "because the act undermines American civilization." Here is Prager on the essential character of American civilization: "The United States of America is the only country in history to have defined itself as Judeo-Christian."[14]

In his book *The Case for Islamo-Christian Civilization*, the historian Richard Bulliet offers a list of fractures, disputes, and violent conflicts between Protestants, Catholics, and Jews and notes, "Protestants and Catholics may have butchered one another in the past, and Christians may have massacred and vilified Jews and been feared and despised in return, but our appreciation—today—of civilizational kinship among Protestants, Catholics and Jews is immune to such unfortunate historical memories."[15] Instead, we choose to center the theological resonances and positive historical memories between these groups, forming them into a narrative that animates and unites "the West."

Donald Trump has unwittingly highlighted at least one of these theological disputes by proclaiming that standing up for Judeo-Christian values will mean Americans can start saying "Merry Christmas" again. Jews, of course, do not celebrate Christmas as a religious holiday.[16]

Bulliet convincingly shows that there are at least as many theological resonances and moments of historical connection between Islam and Christianity (and, for that matter, Islam and Judaism) as there are between Christianity and Judaism. These include everything from revealed sacred texts to prophetic figures to the idea that believing in God and taking care of your neighbor are connected. So if the ugliness can be buried and the resonances lifted up between the first two of the three great monotheisms such that they can somehow be talked about as a single civilization (one whose primary purpose these days seems to be to exclude adherents of the third), why not attempt a different combination? The chief obstacle, Bulliet claims, is "a historical master narrative rooted in fourteen centuries of fear and polemic, and, of course, the current conviction among many Westerners that there is something 'wrong' with Islam."[17]

Lucky for us, we live in the United States, a nation whose national narrative is constantly being expanded by new voices and whose civil society is shaped by the hands of its citizens. The history just sketched highlights an inspiring opportunity. If the dynamics of American religious diversity changed so vastly in the past, through the launch of a new civil religion narrative in the form of the "Judeo-Christian" ideal and efforts to align the national reality with the new ideal, can a similar process occur again? And what might that look like now, when Muslims are the group around which controversy swirls?

In the previous chapter, I wrote about the legal resistance to Trump's anti-Muslim policies and the growing energy of Trump-era interfaith movements that seek to create a wider sense of "we." But for a new civil religion narrative with the force of "Judeo-Christian America" to emerge, interfaith activists are going to need to find stories that match the intensity of that of the Four Chaplains, stories that dramatize both the heroism of American Muslims and the contributions that they make to the nation, stories that form an archetype in the American imagination that can replace the image of Muslim-as-terrorist.

Thankfully, such narratives abound. There are, for example, several stories of Muslims who were victims of white supremacist violence and forgave their assailants, even going so far as to beg the courts for mercy on their behalf. One such story is the case of Raisuddin Bhuiyan, a Bangladeshi American Muslim who was working at a gas station in Texas on September 21, 2001, when a man named Mark Stroman, who described himself as an "allied combatant . . . out hunting Arabs," shot him in the face. As told expertly by Anand Giridharadas in *The True American*, Bhuiyan forgave his attacker in the name of Islam, then waged a battle against the Texas courts to save Stroman from execution.[18]

Here is another story connected to the events of 9/11. Mohammad Salman Hamdani, a twenty-three-year-old Muslim American New Yorker born in Pakistan, disappeared with thousands of others on September 11, 2001. He had been on his way to work at a DNA analysis lab at Rockefeller University. Hamdani was a police cadet, a certified medical technician, and a volunteer for an ambulance service. None of that seemed to matter to the authorities after 9/11. They viewed him principally as a suspect. As his family searched frantically for him, the police were circulating flyers with his picture that said, "Hold and detain. Notify: major case squad."

For six harrowing months, a cloud of suspicion hung over Hamdani's reputation, intensifying his family's grief. It wasn't until March 2002 that his name was cleared. It turns out that Hamdani, upon seeing the planes hit the World Trade Center, had run toward the disaster, hoping to help his fellow Americans. His body was found in the wreckage near the remains of other first responders.

Several officials acknowledged Hamdani in public ways, including Representative Keith Ellison and New York City police chief Raymond Kelly. He was buried in a New York Police Department ceremony. Mayor Michael Bloomberg spoke of him with awe, saying, "Salman stood up when most people would have gone in the other direction."

But, unlike in the case of the Four Chaplains, Hamdani has been denied some of the recognition that many think should be his due, given the combination of heroic sacrifice and prejudice-driven suspicion. The most important slight is his not being included as one of the fallen first responders on the National September 11 Memorial.

His mother believes it is because of his first name. "They don't want someone with the name Mohammad to be up there."[19]

Who would not sympathize with Mrs. Hamdani, after all that she has been through? And who would not understand, by extension, the pain of Muslims in America, the pain of feeling that your name will never be honored by your nation?

And yet, the belief that America would never give full honors to a man named Muhammad is not entirely true.

In 1966, a championship boxer once known as Cassius Clay claimed that his adopted religion, Islam, forbade him from fighting in America's war in Vietnam. After winning a boxing match by knockout in the seventh round, the man who had taken the name Muhammad Ali told television cameras, "My conscience won't let me go shoot my brother, or some darker people, or some poor hungry people in the mud for big powerful America."

A year later, in Houston, Ali formally refused to be inducted into the armed services. He was convicted of a felony, stripped of his boxing license, fined, and sentenced to jail.

At the time, the vast majority of the American public reviled Ali for his position. Certainly, his Muslim name contributed to their loathing. The American television host David Susskind called Ali a disgrace to his country, his race, and his profession. Even Jackie Robinson criticized him.

The law of the land, the Supreme Court, stood up for Ali. They vacated the decision of the lower court, paving the way for Ali to start boxing widely again. The Court took seriously his faith-based conscientious objector claim, which means they took seriously his faith.[20]

It took time, but America ultimately stood up for Ali. By the time he returned to the spotlight and the ring, Ali had lost three prime years of his boxing career, but his personality was just as large and joyous. He argued with reporters, he cracked jokes at press conferences, and he provoked challengers, often in rhyme. He won boxing matches, and he lost some as well. Along the way he became a beloved icon, in this country and beyond. The BBC named Ali the Sports Personality of the Century.

Perhaps most poignantly, he was selected to light the Olympic Cauldron at the Centennial Games in Atlanta in 1996. Remarkably, the choice had been kept a secret from the world. Even the athletes who were participating in the opening ceremony did not know that Muhammad Ali had been given the ultimate honor.

Let us remember how the scene unfolded. Here is Janet Evans, the great swimmer, running the torch up the ramp. She does not know who will take it from her hands. As if by magic, the Champ appears on the Olympic Stage. He takes the flame and stands there for a moment, holding the torch high. The announcers almost do not know what to say, the cameras flash and flash, the applause of the stadium is thunderous. And there is Ali, his body shaking with Parkinson's disease, his face glowing, receiving the acclaim of a nation that once viewed him as a traitor and refused to call him by his Muslim name.[21]

It is precisely the full-circle quality of the story that makes this a civil religion moment for American Muslims.

When Muhammad Ali died in early June 2016, he was given what can only be described as a state funeral. The ceremony was carried live on both news and sports channels. Celebrities and senior officials made statements or were present in person. Several commented on Ali's Muslim faith and the role it played in his refusal to fight in Vietnam. Attorney General Eric Holder said, "His biggest win came not in the ring but in our courts in his fight for his beliefs."[22]

President Barack Obama spoke of Ali's conviction and its influence on the nation: "It would earn him enemies on the left and the right, make him reviled, and nearly send him to jail. But Ali stood his ground. And his victory helped us get used to the America we recognize today."[23]

My favorite story at Ali's funeral was told by the comedian Billy Crystal.

Once, when Crystal was visiting Ali's hometown of Louisville, the boxer invited the comedian to join him on a run at the country club where he exercised. Crystal had to decline. Why? Ali demanded to know. Afraid you can't keep up with the Champ? The real answer was far more depressing. The country club did not admit Jews.

Ali was incensed. Racism and religious bigotry enraged him no matter who was being targeted. He declared that he would never set foot in that country club again.

That was, in part at least, Ali's Muslim conviction speaking. Just as his Muslim faith moved him to stand his ground on the Vietnam War, so it moved him to stand up for a Jew in Louisville.

People change America, people with all kinds of faiths and names, including the name Muhammad.

5

The American *Ummah* in the Era of Islamophobia

The central argument of this essay is that the defining dynamic of America is diversity. Negotiating the challenge of being one nation with many identity communities is this country's origin, essence, and destiny. But it is important to recognize that the various identity groups that were drawn (in some cases, dragged) to this land and collectively created a country are themselves made up of a variety of smaller identity groups—Italian Catholics and Irish Catholics, Polish Jews and German Jews, Latinos from Guatemala and Latinos from Brazil. If, to paraphrase Walt Whitman, the poetical nature of the United States is determined by the dynamics of engagement *between* those identity communities, then there is also American poetry to be drawn from such dynamics *within* those communities.[1]

This is a story well told by Chaim Potok in his classic novel *The Chosen*.[2] The book is set during the early years of World War II in Brooklyn neighborhoods that contain a mosaic of Jewish communities, all of them Orthodox but each with its own leader, a rabbi who offers a slightly different interpretation of the tradition. The horror of the Holocaust and the United States' involvement in World War II has put pressure on all of these Jews to prove their Americanness. They find themselves organizing intra-Jewish baseball leagues to show that they are physically fit and engaged in the mainstream culture. It is in one of these leagues that Danny and Reuven, the two main characters, drawn from rival Jewish communities led by strong men who happen to be their fathers, meet and become friends.

The plot pivots on an array of arguments that characterize Jewish American identity among these particular communities in the 1940s—the proper way to raise children, the best strategy to ensure the continuity of the tradition, whether to support the emerging state of Israel. The two rabbis at the center of the book disagree sharply on nearly all of these matters. Danny's father, the more conservative of the two, denounces the views of Reuven's father to the broader community on several occasions, and he even goes so far as to forbid his son Danny from continuing his friendship with Reuven.

All the while, Reuven's father patiently encourages his son to sympathize with Danny's father's worldview, even while Danny's father openly criticizes him. The fierce devotion of men like Danny's father carried Jewish communities through the pogroms and created space for Orthodox Judaism in America. One can disagree with the current expressions of their devotion, Reuven's father tells his son, while at the same time appreciating its source.

It is interesting to note that Potok places many of the scenes in his novel in quintessentially American spaces such as the baseball diamond and the public library. The symbolism is clear: what these Jews are doing in negotiating their internal differences and creating a larger sense of Jewish identity is a profoundly American story.

Like many Americans, I read the book when I was a high school student. Even at that age, I was deeply struck by a single feature of the novel. None of the events would have taken place—not the intra-Jewish baseball game, nor the friendship between Danny and Reuven, nor the sympathetic explanations from Reuven's father about the actions of other rabbis—had it not been for the anti-Semitism of that era. It was prejudice that forced rival, insular communities of

American Jews to engage with each other to create what we now think of as American Judaism.

As it was with Jews in *The Chosen*, so it is with Muslims now. No nation on earth has a Muslim community that is more ethnically, racially, or theologically diverse than that in the United States. For many years, those various Muslim groups created separate spaces— mosques, schools, community centers, and so on. Those who were less ritualistically observant often found no space at all. The era of Islamophobia has forced them all together and raised fascinating questions about what it means to be American, what it means to be Muslim (*ummah* means Muslim community), and who gets to define the identity American Muslim.

Consider the example of Aziz Ansari. Ansari is a highly successful actor, writer, stand-up comic, and director born to Indian Muslim parents. He hosted *Saturday Night Live* the day after Donald Trump's inauguration, and while he is not, by his own admission, the least bit observant as a Muslim, there he was on one of the biggest stages in American life on the second day of Trump's presidency. As the hip-hop kids say, he chose to represent.

Ansari offered lessons in the science of prejudice through a set of humorous stories about Muslims. He made a joke about watching tapes of President George W. Bush's speeches about Islam and experiencing feelings of nostalgia for a man he once considered— I am quoting directly—"a dildo." He reminded his audience that Muslims worship the same God as Christians and Jews. If you just changed the music on *Homeland*, he joked, we wouldn't look so scary.

In a *New York Times* op-ed published a few months earlier, Ansari wrote about several of the same themes, but this time through the poignant story of instructing his parents not to go to the mosque for prayer lest they wind up the victims of an Islamophobic attack.[3]

So far, so good. Muslim community leaders most certainly want American Muslim public figures, whether observant or not, to speak out against Islamophobia and offer basic knowledge about the religion. The bigger the stage, the better.

But then season two of Ansari's highly successful Netflix series *Master of None* came out, and one of the episodes was titled "Religion." The opening scenes include a shot of a young Ansari, in his role as Dev, gleefully continuing to eat bacon at a friend's breakfast table right after getting a phone call from his mother reminding him that pork is forbidden for Muslims. The scene cuts to Dev's father pleading with him to pretend to the religiously observant family friends who are visiting that he is fasting for Ramadan and is punctilious about making his five daily prayers at the correct times. Dev responds by convincing *their* son *not* to fast and, moreover, to skip the Eid prayer and indulge in pork barbeque at a festival in Brooklyn instead.

When Dev orders pork at a dinner out with his parents and their religiously observant friends, his exasperated mother can't take it anymore and stops talking to him. Dev doesn't understand why she's so mad. His father explains: teaching religion is a way of both caring for your children and continuing a tradition. Dev is being dismissive about both values. Chastened, Dev opens the Qur'an his mother gave him when he was a child, finds a verse he likes, and texts it to his mother: "To you your religion and to me mine."

The episode closes with alternating scenes of Dev's parents offering greetings to diverse Muslims after congregational prayer and Dev offering greetings to his diverse friends at what appears to be a wine tasting for hipster New Yorkers.[4]

On the one hand, this is terrific. Not only does it add to the voices speaking out against Islamophobia, it increases the number of nonterrorist Muslims that Americans can identify. Moreover, it gives the lie to the Islamophobe's claim that all Muslims are the same. Ansari, with his profanity-laced tirades and his jokes about sex, is certainly not like the bearded imam at the local mosque.

But what do observant Muslims do when one of the most prominent defenders of Muslims in the public square is producing

shows that encourage Muslims to skip Eid to go eat pork at a barbeque festival and suggesting that the fellowship of a wine tasting is
comparable to the fellowship at *jummah* prayers? Somewhere in
America, a fourteen-year-old Muslim kid has lied to his parents and
said he is going to his room to offer the dusk prayer, and is instead
watching the "Religion" episode from Ansari's show and laughing
hysterically. And in the kitchen of that household, there are a Muslim mother and father whose highest hope is that their kids walk
what Muslims call *sirat al mustaqeem* (the straight path), and they
are *scared out of their minds.*[5]

The literary critic Leon Wieseltier once observed (I paraphrase)
that on September 10, 2001, nobody in America seemed to be talking about Islam; on September 12, 2001, everybody in America
seemed to be talking about Islam.[6]

   This is not actually true. At least one group of people in America was talking about Islam before September 10, 2001: Muslims
involved in internal Muslim institutions. By *internal Muslim institutions*
I mean spaces like mosques, Muslim schools, and Muslim community organizations such as the Islamic Society of North America
(ISNA), institutions whose primary purpose is to shape Muslim
identity. The leaders of these groups derived their authority from
their piety, their knowledge of the tradition, and their advocacy of a
narrow set of international issues (here I refer to immigrant Muslims mainly; African American Muslims have long advocated for a
broader set of concerns), chiefly the Palestinian cause. Generally
speaking, these Muslim leaders had the stage to themselves. They
tended to be on the conservative side of the spectrum, and their
focus was almost entirely ritual observance—doing the daily
prayers, reading the Qur'an, fasting for Ramadan, and maintaining
Muslim lifestyle values, which are virtually indistinguishable from
the lifestyle values derived from theologically conservative interpretations of other major world religions, especially when it comes
to matters of sexual expression. These leaders grumbled occasion-

ally about America, mainly for its R-rated popular culture and its pro-Israel foreign policy, but mostly their attention was focused on trying to make their kids Muslim in the way that they themselves were Muslim.

Let me tell a personal story that illustrates this point. After serving on a panel with a group of highly respected Muslim scholars at the ISNA convention a few years ago and feeling pretty good about my performance, I was a bit taken aback when one of the audience members, a middle-aged woman wearing a headscarf, chased me down in the hallway after the session and demanded I remove my earrings. I must have given her a confused look, so she helpfully explained her reasoning: "I tell my teenage sons that being a good Muslim is not doing things the Americans do like boys wearing earrings. You shouldn't be wearing those at ISNA. Does your mother know you wear them? YOU SHOULDN'T BE WEARING EARRINGS AT ALL."

By the end, her voice had risen to a shout. About a dozen people turned to stare at the commotion. Nobody looked especially surprised to see a fifty-something-year-old mother admonishing a thirty-something-year-old man about wearing earrings.

A consequence of attempting to keep an identity pure through social control is that a set of people will declare themselves deviants and leave. A consequence of powerful outsiders attacking an identity is that people with even the slimmest connection to that identity will feel offended, find that once-small part of themselves growing in personal significance, then seek to reconnect with that identity, often by playing some role of value for that identity community. This is what appears to have happened with Ansari, who, before recent events, had rarely, if ever, mentioned his Muslim heritage in public. A *New Yorker* profile published a few years before did not make a single reference to it.[7] The era of Islamophobia woke that part of him up. And he is not the only one. Consider the story of the writer and comedian Zahra Noorbakhsh.

For many years, Noorbakhsh did a stand-up routine in which she jokingly referred to herself as the "pork-eating, alcohol-drinking

kind of Muslim." She had tired of Muslim ritual practice as a child
and didn't like the sexism of the tradition or the community. She
effectively declared herself a deviant and walked away. In an essay
for the National Public Radio program *Fresh Air*, Noorbakhsh described how the election of Trump made her want to learn Muslim
prayers again, to reconnect with the tradition and community in
which she was raised, and to defend it.[8]

More and more Muslims like Ansari and Noorbakhsh are becom-
ing more and more visible. There are plenty of writers, performers,
and other types of storytellers in this group, including figures like
Reza Aslan, Wajahat Ali, Omid Safi, Hasan Minhaj, G. Willow Wilson,
Nura Afia, Ayad Akhtar, Yasiin Bey (formerly Mos Def), Mahershala
Ali, Mona Haydar, Dave Chappelle, and Mona Eltahawy. But there
are also figures in the areas of law and policy like Farhana Khera,
Ilhan Omar, Shaarik Zafar, Farah Pandith, Abdul El-Sayed, and
Zeenat Rahman, as well as civil society leaders like Kashif Sheikh,
Nadia Roumani, Farhan Latif, Daisy Khan, and Linda Sarsour, who
would be in this group. If you needed to put me somewhere, it
would probably be here.

There are certainly enough such Muslims to consider whether
we form something of a sociological category, especially vis-à-vis
the kind of Muslims described earlier, the ones who created and
defined what I call "internal Muslim spaces." It seems to me that the
most useful distinction between the two groups is that people like
Ansari and Noorbakhsh view themselves (and are viewed by others)
as principally interpreting the contemporary Muslim social experience, whereas the Muslims who create internal Muslim spaces view
themselves (and are viewed by others) as principally interpreting
the Islamic tradition, meaning the Qur'an, the hadith, and figures in
Islamic law and philosophy. For the time being, let us call the Ansari
types "social Muslims" and the people who start mosques "traditional
Muslims."

The most significant distinctions between social Muslims and
traditional Muslims are about sources of authority, the spaces they

tend to occupy, and the topics on which they most frequently focus. Traditional Muslims derive their authority from knowledge of sacred sources and vocal emphasis on personal piety. Social Muslims derive their authority from their ability to create positive impressions about Muslims for the broader society. The individual who gives a sermon during Friday prayers at the mosque, or some other kind of internal Muslim space, is likely to be a traditional Muslim. The person being interviewed on CNN, doing stand-up comedy in a club, or writing an op-ed for the *New York Times* is most likely to be a social Muslim. There are, of course, a set of people who straddle categories—Dalia Mogahed, Khalid Latif, Sherman Jackson, Rami Nashashibi, Maha Elgenaidi, Imam Mohamed Magid, Jenan Mohajir, Imam Feisal Abdul Rauf, Imam Zaid Shakir, Hamza Yusuf, Haroon Moghul, and Ahmed Rehab, to name a few. But, generally speaking, Ansari is not likely to be found at the *minbar* (pulpit in a mosque), and the *khatib* (Muslim preacher) has a difficult time telling stories about the Muslim social experience in a manner that the CNN audience understands. He is certainly not doing stand-up comedy in a club.

In my mind, the most interesting part of the "social Muslim" category is that it is, in large part at least, created by Islamophobia. This is the case for two reasons. I have already commented on the first—the singling out of Muslim identity in the atmosphere of Islamophobia had the effect of increasing in salience what was once a small, even dormant, piece of identity in people like Ansari and Noorbakhsh.

But creating a discourse requires both people willing to speak and people interested in listening, and in our time, the desire by the growing number of social Muslims to speak up *as* Muslims is matched by the growing interest in stories *about* Muslims. In other words, the second way in which Islamophobia created the "social Muslim" category is by supplying it a stage and an audience.

The type of stage where these stories tend to appear—Netflix, the *New York Times*, NPR, CNN, Comedy Central, Judd Apatow films—is important to note. The *New Yorker* in the Trump era alone has run pieces on a Muslim poet, a Muslim cop, a Muslim lawyer, a Muslim comedian, and a Muslim tamale vendor.

Such outlets are, of course, associated with urban, multicultural, progressive Whole Foods America; not so much white, rural, conservative Cracker Barrel America. One gets the sense that if Trump's America insists on casting Muslims as villains and seeking out (or making up) characters who fit the bill, then Barack Obama's America will respond by promoting Muslims whom they consider heroes. In fact, Whole Foods America is equally adept at inventing Muslim characters who live up to our heroic multicultural fantasies—behold the new best-selling comic book series Ms. Marvel, which is about a Pakistani American Muslim female superhero who lives in New Jersey.[9]

Muslims, in other words, have become a totem in the current chapter of the American culture wars, a symbol that signals, above all, a tribal belonging (Trump/red/rural/evangelical/Cracker Barrel versus Obama/blue/urban/secular/Whole Foods), with each tribe doing its best to foist on the category "Muslim" its preferred set of characteristics. There is no better illustration of this than the Shepard Fairey poster, made for his series *We the People*, that features a steely-eyed woman wearing bright red lipstick and an American flag hijab. For Whole Foods America, Muslim women have become the visual symbol of anti-Trump progressive multiculturalism.

And there is no better embodiment of that poster than Linda Sarsour. A Palestinian American Muslim activist and mother of three, Sarsour became the most visible organizer of the National Women's March, which drew over a million people to the National Mall on the day after Trump was inaugurated. A powerful speaker whose signature lines include "Fear is a choice" and "I am unapologetically Palestinian, Muslim, and from Brooklyn," Sarsour became, in the opening months of 2017, perhaps the most recognizable symbol of the anti-Trump resistance in American life. She was a living representation of the Fairey image.

Sarsour's story unfolds like a template of the identity politics movement. Born in Brooklyn in 1980, the eldest of seven in a Palestinian American immigrant family, Sarsour went to a highly racially diverse school in the Sunset Park neighborhood and translated for her non-English-speaking immigrant mother in doctors' offices and grocery stores.[10]

After 9/11, Sarsour began working at the Arab American Association of New York, and she found herself politicized by the anti-Muslim and anti-Arab policies (everything from the Patriot Act to the Iraq War) advanced by the Bush administration. Her own childhood in multicultural Brooklyn helped her connect the experiences of Arabs and Muslims to those of other people of color. She explains her evolving consciousness to the *Fader*: "People were like, 'Linda, this apparatus, this racial profiling that you're speaking of is impacting immigrant communities, black communities.' . . . I finally realized that my community was just an additional community being targeted."[11]

Sarsour began to take visible leadership roles in a range of activist efforts, from organizing New York's highly diverse Muslim communities to advocate for Eid to be an official holiday to protesting the NYPD's controversial surveillance program targeting Muslims. The murder of Michael Brown by a police officer in Ferguson in 2014 further radicalized Sarsour's politics, and her involvement in protests there strengthened her relationship with a range of national-level activists. They recognized in her a uniquely gifted organizer and public voice who also occupied a set of highly desirable progressive identities (Palestinian, Muslim, female, Brooklyn hipster). She was a natural choice to cochair the Women's March, and she made the most of the opportunity.

In the aftermath of the march, Linda managed to court the right amount of controversy to ensure she stayed in the public eye. When a group of right-wing activists (in fact, many of the same people who had publicly opposed Cordoba House) loudly protested her selection as a commencement speaker at the City University of

New York because of her criticism of Israel, Sarsour deftly turned the tables on them, becoming a symbol for everyone from liberal Jews to conservative Muslims to rally around. The *New York Times*[12] reported on the hubbub, and *Time Magazine* posted both a video and the full transcript of her commencement address, which was textbook twenty-first-century progressive identity politics: "We in this room must commit to never being bystanders to poverty, lack of jobs and healthcare, sexism, violence, discrimination, racism, xenophobia, Islamophobia, anti-Semitism, and homophobia." Sarsour took in her standing ovation with a defiant fist raised in the air.[13]

Sarsour was asked to cochair the Women's March under the banner of embracing intersectionality, at least as it is typically understood within the progressive identity politics paradigm. Sarsour's comments in her CUNY commencement speech and at the Women's March fit squarely within that worldview ("follow women of color" was one of her Women's March rallying cries).

But at least one important identity group was actively marginalized at the Women's March: pro-life advocates, including pro-life women's groups. The Women's March had an explicitly pro-choice platform and prominent pro-choice financial support, and its organizers had actually proactively disinvited a pro-life women's group from the sponsorship circle.

What is interesting about this is that most Islamic scholars, and by extension most traditional Muslims, are pro-life. As in other religions, there are nuances and exceptions, but generally speaking abortion is viewed as wrong and forbidden.[14]

In fact, traditional Muslim leaders and scholars have typically been far more comfortable with the pro-life side of the American culture wars, alongside American social conservatives, than with the pro-choice side and American liberals. They are more aligned, for example, with an identity politics that advances "traditional families" and religious freedom than with one that seeks transgender bathrooms. As Sarsour has been rallying women of color at progressive demonstrations and appearing on stage with LGBT icons,[15] Shaykh Hamza Yusuf, one of American Islam's most prominent and respected traditional Muslim scholars, has been speaking about religious freedom at several universities with Princeton's Robert George, one of the most influential conservative Catholic intellectuals in the United States.[16]

I doubt Shaykh Hamza would take much comfort from seeing signs that say "Immigrants and Muslims Welcome" on the doors of gay bars and sex shops. In fact, he might well point out that the tribe of identity-politics progressives that has, of late, embraced Muslims has done so more out of a hatred of Trump than any knowledge of Islam. The real danger of this dynamic for traditional Muslims is not necessarily what non-Muslims think of Islam but rather what Muslims think about it. As social Muslims grow in numbers and migrate into the warm embrace of identity-politics progressives based on the experience of marginalization, the more the contaminants of progressive politics will inevitably seep into what ought to be the pure waters of Islam.

All of this is to say that while Muslims are changing America, present-day America is changing the Muslim community. For traditional Muslims, the dynamics of the era of Islamophobia present severe complications. For the longest time, they had the topic of Islam to themselves. They could present it to their children the way they wanted to. Yes, American culture was cacophonous and sexually explicit, but they could say, "We Muslims are not like *them*." And when something felt out of place, like, say, a young male speaker at ISNA with earrings, they could scold him in the hallways, thereby exerting social control, cleansing the space, and keeping the identity pure. But what do you do when it feels as though you are being given a choice between keeping the identity pure and keeping your children safe? Ansari, by creating a positive impression of Muslims in a large segment of America, obviously helps with the latter, but he does it by compromising the former.

For me, it is a distinctly American metaphor that best helps make sense of this dynamic—namely, the city on a hill. It is a phrase that first appeared in the Bible, and that John Winthrop invoked to his compatriots aboard the *Arabella*, offering them a symbol to visualize the character he hoped his Massachusetts Bay settlement would embody. Over the course of the twentieth century—through speeches by the likes of John F. Kennedy, Ronald Reagan, and Obama—Americans have come to think of the City on a Hill as a symbol of pluralism. Reagan spoke of it thus in his farewell speech: "a tall, proud city . . . teeming with people of all kinds living in harmony and peace . . . the doors . . . open to anyone with the will and the heart to get here."[17]

That is not the City on a Hill that Winthrop imagined or, in fact, built. As Peter Manseau points out in his excellent book *One Nation, under Gods*, Winthrop's "godly community in the supposed godless wilderness" allowed only one religious opinion, enforced purity through civil authority, and punished dissenters.[18] Manseau argues that Winthrop's deepest concern was that his city would be "swallowed by the waves of competing religious ideas . . . all around them."[19]

Just as Kennedy, Reagan, and Obama spoke proudly of the diversity of the modern American city on a hill, so did Winthrop speak proudly of the purity of his symbolic city. He intended for it to be "a bulwark against the kingdom of the Anti-Christ,"[20] by which he meant the Roman Catholic Church. He warned against the seduction of worshiping other gods. He banished those who developed different interpretations about Christianity, most famously Roger Williams and Anne Hutchinson.

Traditional Muslims have more in common with the early Puritans than identity-politics progressives might like to admit. Many of the internal Muslim institutions that they established emphasized purity, were bulwarks against religious diversity, and did not take kindly to what the Puritans referred to as "strange opinions," otherwise known as alternative interpretations of a religious tradition.

But in the era of Islamophobia, Muslims by and large found that American diversity language was their best chance at establishing a safe neighborhood within the national city. And so people who wanted to establish their City on a Hill on the Winthrop model of purity found that they needed to invoke the Kennedy/Reagan/ Obama "city of diversity" in order to have a place. And once you invoke diversity as a value that gives you a place in the larger city, it is hard to turn around and deny a place to people (gay Muslims, Shia Muslims, non-hijabi female Muslims, less-observant-than-you Muslims) who demand a similar safety in your neighborhood based on that same value.

Especially when those people are doing work that benefits you.

My wife has an interesting story along these lines. Like Noorbakhsh, she felt repelled by the second-class status of women in Muslim institutions as an adolescent, so she stopped participating in them. Unlike Noorbakhsh, she remained connected to the religious tradition and held fast to her Muslim identity; she just never went to a mosque. The way her faith principally expressed itself was in her choice of profession, civil rights attorney. In the aftermath of 9/11, my wife was approached by a conservative Muslim group who asked that she defend them in a case in which the city council was raising what they believed were unfair and discriminatory issues about a building they had purchased and planned to convert into a mosque and Muslim school. My wife took the case, wore her typical attire to court (skirt suits, no headscarf), gritted her teeth when the leader of the community looked uncomfortable while shaking her hand (many religiously traditional Muslims, like religiously traditional Jews, eschew touching a non–family member of the opposite gender), and often joked about the irony of fighting for the establishment of a mosque that she would not want to pray in and that would likely not welcome her in the first place.

There is a scene in the documentary *The Muslims Are Coming!* in which a related tension flares into the open.[21] The film documents a group of Muslim comedians touring the American South, performing for largely rural white audiences who are meeting real, live Muslims for the first time. At one of their shows, the audience is more diverse. A group of adolescent Muslim girls from an Islamic school have driven in to see the show. Dressed modestly in Islamic headscarves, you can see them begin to shift uncomfortably when one of the female comedians, Negin Farsad, starts telling jokes about her sex life. Finally, one of the girls from the Islamic school gives the signal, and they walk out while Farsad is in the middle of a sentence.

It is a tense scene, made even more tense when Farsad says, in her on-camera reflection after the incident, that Islam and Muslims are not as good on gender and sexuality issues as she wants them to be.

It made me wonder what those Muslim girls from the Islamic school were saying about her. The filmmakers, notably, did not capture their take on the situation. The film was being made for Whole Foods America, a cultural sect that identifies far more with Farsad's approach to gender, sexuality, religion, and identity than those girls from the Islamic school did.

What interests me is that Farsad and those girls were in the same scene at all. For the longest time, those girls claimed the space of Islam and left comedy stages to Farsad. But now those girls needed Farsad. Her routine, after all, was building positive awareness about Islam and Muslims within an audience that might come to those girls' defense if their Islamic school were ever attacked. The price of that defense, however, was Farsad's desire to have a say in the world of Muslim identity. In other words, Farsad may have been improving the attitudes of a certain set of Americans toward Islam and Muslims, but she was doing it in a way that many Muslims would feel distorted the values of their tradition and community.

I have spent most of this chapter on the tensions between traditional and social Muslims. But there are many other identity groups within American Islam and a whole range of interactions that the era of Islamophobia is forcing. Consider this story. In 2017, the Academy Award for Best Supporting Actor went to Mahershala Ali, an American Muslim, for his role in the film *Moonlight*. It was the first time a Muslim had won an Oscar. Pakistan's envoy to the United Nations sent out a congratulatory tweet, then deleted it. Why? Because Ali is part of the Ahmadiyya community, which is not considered Muslim according to the Pakistani Constitution. Ahmadis have certain beliefs that deviate from mainstream Muslim doctrine. As a result, Pakistan amended its constitution to declare the community non-Muslim, forbidding them from uttering Islamic prayers in public or call their houses of worship mosques.

Pakistan is not alone in its view that Ahmadis are dangerous, blaspheming heretics. Ahmadis are not legally allowed into the Muslim holy cities of Mecca and Medina, even for the annual Hajj pilgrimage. Barring a Muslim community from the Hajj, with the support of a vast array of other Muslims? That is a stunning and, in my view, deeply bigoted position.

While it is likely the case that many traditional Muslims in America view the distinctive practices and beliefs of Ahmadis as heretical, there were very few public displays of disparagement toward Ali. A month earlier, Ali had won the Screen Actors Guild Award for his role in *Moonlight*, and he had given an impassioned speech about being a proud Muslim and the need to build welcoming communities across lines of difference in America. Whatever some Muslims in America might feel about Ahmadi doctrine and practices, were they really going to criticize a highly accomplished actor for standing up for Muslims because they didn't like his doctrine, especially in the immediate aftermath of the Muslim ban?

For his part, Ali did not use the stage given to him by his awards to make a case for Ahmadi rights, or to denounce the Muslims around the world who deny them, even though many of the Ahmadis who come to the United States from countries like Pakistan come as religious refugees, fleeing persecution by other Muslims in those countries. Ali chose, instead, to represent himself simply as a

Muslim, doing a great service to others who hold that identity and, along the way, expanding who that category includes.

My statement that there was not an outpouring of public disparagement about Ali should not mask another important fact: there was also not a broad outpouring of support. It's not like Muslims were putting up billboards with Ali's image or engaging in large-scale public celebrations of his win.

This might be partially because of the minority Muslim theological community to which Ali belongs. But that is likely not the only reason. In addition to being Ahmadi, Ali is black. As Sarah Harvard highlights in a *Washington Post* piece, immigrant Muslims who won creative awards in the Trump era—namely, Ansari and Riz Ahmed— were far more celebrated by Muslim groups than African American Muslims—like Ali and Dave Chappelle—who won similar awards.[22]

Scholars like Su'ad Abdul Khabeer and Zaid Abdullah view this as part of a central dynamic within the broader American Muslim community. "Muslim immigrants come over empowered in a particular way, they come over with resources we didn't have, and they also didn't have the social stigma many African Americans had. We cannot compare African American Muslims with South Asian or immigrant Muslims, because we're on two separate class levels."[23]

Of all the diversity negotiations within the Muslim community, the one around race may be the most fraught and, therefore, the most American. After all, it is a challenge that the community shares with its nation.

6

IMAN

A lia Bilal is the daughter of African American parents who converted to Islam in the 1970s. Her family lived in a largely African American neighborhood on the South Side of Chicago, but Alia was sent to an Islamic school with a predominantly Arab American population in the majority-white southern suburbs. Alia describes the school as having been warm and welcoming, while at the same time being a bit unsettling. She could not help but notice how the neighborhoods changed markedly as she crossed from the city into the suburbs, or that the parents of her friends at the Islamic school had professional jobs that allowed them economic entry into the white suburbs even as they built a separate socioreligious bunker for themselves. And while the school frequently talked about the importance of service and mercy in Islam, and organized fund-raising campaigns and clothing drives to implement these values, the appeals were always made for causes outside the United States, and the resources were typically sent abroad. Her own neighborhood could use some of those material resources, Alia would think to herself. She would never dare to share those thoughts at her school, though. She was embarrassed about living on the wrong side of the economic divide. She also got the sense that the people at her school looked down on her neighborhood in other ways. Not only was her community seen as an economic failure, she had the sense that it was also viewed as culturally impure.

Alia's experience is a window onto a set of critical tensions within the American Muslim community. Their main associations (the Islamic Society of North America for immigrant-born Muslims, the Mosque Cares for African American Muslims) used to hold their annual conventions in the same city (Chicago) over the same weekend (Labor Day) and barely acknowledge that the other existed. African American Muslims accused immigrant Muslims of adopting a superior attitude when it came to the practice of Islam and focusing too much on "back home" concerns while ignoring the very real problems of poverty and racism that existed in America, problems that largely affected African Americans and that immigrant Muslims did their best to escape by moving to leafy suburbs and building enveloping and exclusionary institutions. And they were right: immigrant Muslims were in fact guilty of all of these things.

Scholars like Su'ad Abdul Khabeer point out that when the immigrant narrative dominates, the African American Muslim experience is often erased from the picture. "Under these ideological guidelines," writes Khabeer, "a Muslim of Arab descent, for example, is presumed to have proximity to the Islamic tradition, and her religious practices and perspectives are endowed with authenticity simply because she is Arab. By contrast, a Muslim who cannot claim immediate descent from the 'Muslim world,' such as a U.S. Black American, is presumed to be new to the Islamic tradition, and her religious practices and perspectives have to be authenticated."[1]

I have some insight into at least one version of the immigrant Muslim worldview, given my own (fitful, for sure) formation in a South Asian Ismaili Muslim community in Chicago. Its leaders (which included my parents, also fitfully) were desperately trying to build a set of institutions that allowed them to feel at home in a foreign land and would reproduce their patterns of believing, behaving, and belonging among their children. Convinced that real life and true religion were back home, but being physically located in the United States, they harangued about the myriad impurities of over here while singing the praises of over there. This left their children in an impossible position. The second generation grew up comfortable in the cultural forms of over here while constantly hearing them denounced as profane by their parents. Because so much American popular culture (music, fashion, sports, and so on) is dominated by black people, and because immigrants might be slow at learning English but are lightning quick to understand the many functions of antiblack racism, the manner in which Muslim immigrants distanced themselves from America was by denouncing black expressive culture. In my own household, this took the form of alarm bells ringing on account of my interest in breakdancing. My parents' chief concern was not that I might, given my clumsiness, injure myself badly; it was that my admiration for a black cultural form symbolized both my distance from the religious community and my proximity to the profane elements of American culture.

There was something profoundly self-serving in this attitude. Basically, the story went as follows: To be economically successful in the United States was a sign of virtue, because America was a meritocracy. To be religiously and socially separate was also a sign of virtue, because America was a cesspool of cultural filth.

Of course, immigrant Muslims were unwittingly setting themselves up for a signal danger. As they distanced themselves culturally from the United States, and benefited from it economically, what if people on the other side of that chasm took their discourse at face value? What if Americans said, if you find the culture of this country so profane and the patterns of your homeland so holy, you are very welcome to leave?

It was only after 9/11—when their faith, their institutions, and their citizenship were threatened—that immigrant Muslims en masse discovered the need to prove their "Americanness." They quickly found that one of the best ways to do so was to latch themselves to the African American Muslim narrative, as if they had personally come off slave ships and marched for civil rights. Many African American

Muslims were nonplussed by this, pointing out that they had been ignored by immigrants until they became necessary to ensure the immigrants' survival. The exception to this was an organization called IMAN.

In the summer of 1997, when she was still in elementary school, Alia went to an event called Takin' It to the Streets in Marquette Park, a large green space located in the eponymous neighborhood on the Southwest Side of Chicago. People from a range of ethnic, religious, and class backgrounds were relaxing amid music, food, dancing, games, and inspiring religious speeches. It felt like a summer festival crossed with a spiritual revival. The religious language was Islam, but the undergirding culture was African American, and all of it was meant to be inviting—a bridge, not a bunker. The organizers of the event were members of a multiracial collective who called themselves the Inner City Muslim Action Network (IMAN, both an acronym for the name and a term that means "faith"). Alia promised herself that, when she was old enough, she would work for this organization.

The leader of the group was a recent DePaul University graduate named Rami Nashashibi. Rami had grown up in a secular Palestinian/Jordanian American family and majored in English literature and international studies at DePaul. Like a lot of kids in the 1980s, he had gotten into hip-hop music. As a college student, he started to take an interest in the references to Islam in his favorite songs. As he researched them, he discovered profound connections between Islam and the black experience. He started to realize that Muslim identity was a defining feature of the black figures he lionized, from Muhammad Ali to Malcolm X, and that Islam had been present in the New World long before his maternal grandmother immigrated to the United States. Chicago had been a place of settlement for African American Muslims, as it had been for his own Arab American family and the South Asian Muslim students he was meeting at DePaul. Why did none of these communities seemed to know one another? And why were the immigrant Muslim communities either oblivious to or dismissive of the social problems in the inner city, even as they took the social and political challenges "back home" seriously? Worse, some members of these groups were even contributing to urban social problems by engaging in the profoundly un-Islamic activity of owning liquor stores in ghetto neighborhoods. Inspired by Islam's call to be a mercy on all the worlds and moved by the diverse artistic expressions that emerged from the black experience, Rami and his friends formed IMAN in the mid-1990s to bring diverse Muslim communities together to improve the city they all called home: Chicago. They began with a few modest social service projects, then took on the much more ambitious task of organizing a street festival.

One of the effects of that first Takin' It to the Streets was that a group of young Muslims who had their faith formation in siloed ethnoreligious communities (Palestinian, Egyptian, Pakistani, and so on) but participated in broader American culture through spaces like public schools and summer camps found a home in that experience. They wanted Islam to be part of their lives, but not in the old-world cultural forms presented by their parents. They wanted to enact the social values of Islam in the space where their children would be born, not where their grandparents were buried. They no longer wanted to hide their love for hip-hop music or the fact that they had friends from other religions, or Muslim friends who might have different theological interpretations of Islam (Shia or Sufi, for example), or Muslim friends who were less observant—all things that their parents frowned on. The group of core IMAN organizers grew, and the reputation of the collective started to be known in multiple Muslim communities.

The actual projects grew as well, in both size and sophistication. IMAN went from organizing food baskets to creating a free health clinic that served communities of color from the neighborhood and was mainly staffed by volunteers who were second-generation Arab and South Asian American Muslim immigrants, many of whom drove in from the suburbs to do their volunteer shift. Takin' It to the Streets became a biennial event, attracting top American Muslim artists like Mos Def (now Yasiin Bey) and, on some years, as many as twenty thousand attendees.

Inevitably, IMAN started to interact with other groups doing similar work on the Southwest Side. Patricia Watkins and other black Pentecostal leaders told them that service was all well and good, but it only went so far. To get at the root of the social problems in neighborhoods like Marquette Park, IMAN would need to involve the residents themselves in initiatives that created structural change. And so the IMAN crew started to learn community organizing. One of their initiatives in this category was the corner-store campaign, which encouraged local merchants (many of them Arab American) to carry fresh fruits and vegetables and sell them at affordable prices in a geographic area that was one of the largest food deserts in the United States.

The Jewish Council on Urban Affairs, which also got its start in the Marquette Park neighborhood, saw a parallel to its own work in IMAN. It helped the IMAN leadership think beyond getting individual grants for discrete projects and toward building an institution. And so IMAN formed its first strategic plan and started to purchase property. The staff and budget grew significantly. Alia Bilal fulfilled her promise to herself and joined the IMAN team a dozen years after that first Takin' It to the Streets. She is now senior staff at an organization with a nearly $4 million budget, making it one of the largest American Muslim institutions in the nation.

Because many of the neighborhood groups that IMAN interacted with were also faith based, the topic of religion frequently arose. Once, Rami found himself in a conversation about community development with Rabbi Capers Funnye, the leader of a largely African American synagogue in Marquette Park, about community development when the rabbi realized it was Ramadan. He invited Rami and the IMAN community to do their fast-breaking meal, called an *iftar*, in the synagogue, alongside his largely African American Jewish community.

There were some murmurs of dissent when Rami raised this possibility back at IMAN. Weren't Jews supporters of Israel and therefore the enemies of Muslims? Wouldn't being in a space with Jewish rather than Muslim symbols defile the evening prayers?

Rami was adamantly opposed to this way of thinking. He was not going to allow the work of IMAN, or the residents of Marquette Park, to be held hostage to conflicts abroad, much less petty prejudices here. Moreover, he considered any group with a religious inspiration to improve the neighborhood to be not just a strategic partner but spiritual kin. While Rami, a highly observant and knowledgeable Muslim, knew enough about the Qur'an and Muslim history to cite religious references for these views, he was struck by how quickly other Muslims were convinced about the concept of holding the iftar in the synagogue when they learned that a Muslim leader with a degree from Al-Azhar University (the highly respected Cairo-based institution of Muslim learning) would be leading the prayers. It was a lesson in the importance of recruiting Islamic scholars to vouch for IMAN.

On a sweltering August Saturday in 2016, my family and I made the drive to the Southwest Side for the commemoration of Martin Luther King Jr.'s march in Marquette Park. Fifty years earlier, King, accompanied by seven hundred peaceful marchers, including Archbishop John Cody of Chicago, had marched through this neighborhood calling for fair housing. His efforts drew a crowd of five thousand ethnic whites who screamed racial slurs and hurled bottles and bricks. One famously hit King in the head, sending him to his knees, where he wiped the blood away, stood up, and kept marching.

The moment is captured in a monument that IMAN erected in Marquette Park, the first permanent memorial to King in the city of

Chicago. The monument is made of brick, the material of the homes in Marquette Park and so many other working-class neighborhoods in Chicago. Tiles with images of home, decorated by children in a workshop that IMAN hosted, line one side of the memorial. Two of them belong to my children.

There are quotes from diverse religious leaders on the other side. One is by Rabbi Robert Marx, sharing the story of his experience as an observer of that August march in 1966:

> I saw Catholic priests reviled and nuns spat upon. I found myself—a Rabbi—standing guard like a policeman, over a pile of rocks, for fear that grown men and mothers dragging little children with them, would seize those rocks and throw them at the demonstrators. I saw teenage boys and girls ready to kill. I was on the wrong side of the street. I should have been with the marchers. . . . This afternoon I will join Dr. King and others who will be going back into the area. This time, I will be on the right side of the street.

Rabbi Marx, in part because of that experience, went on to found the Jewish Council on Urban Affairs, the aforementioned group that offered technical assistance to a fledgling IMAN in its early years.

A second quote is by Rami's spiritual hero, Warith Deen Muhammad, who separated from his father's Nation of Islam in the 1970s and led a significant number of African American Muslims into a theologically mainstream Muslim practice that focused on personal responsibility, community uplift, and harmonizing Islam with American culture. Rami tells me that Imam Muhammad is "the most important, least appreciated American Muslim leader of the latter half of the twentieth century."[2] The King memorial eternalizes a line that Imam Muhammad spoke at a Takin' It to the Streets event in 2005 in Marquette Park: "Who is the neighbor now? The neighbor is every nation, the neighbor is every human being. And this is what we want the message of Islam to be in these times. We want it to be the message of unity, the oneness of the human family. We want it to be a message of caring and loving."

Walking in the footsteps of King, listening to the speeches that day, reading the quotes, admiring the monument, and noting how remarkable it was that a Muslim organization started twenty years ago by a handful of local college graduates had just built the first permanent memorial to King in this city, I realized that Rami and IMAN were entering the narrative of American civil religion by offering a new American interpretation of the City on a Hill.

It was an interpretation straight out of Islamic history, but placed seamlessly into the American experience. It was the example of Medina. In the year 622, the Prophet Muhammad and his companions were chased out of their home city of Mecca for preaching a dual message that was deeply disturbing to the status quo—mercy and monotheism. They fled to a city named Yathrib, where the residents welcomed the Prophet and his Companions, who became known as *al muhajiroun*, the immigrants. From that point on, Yahthrib would be known by its new name, Medina, the city of the Prophet. The Ansar, the residents of what was now Medina who had welcomed the Prophet, were accorded a high status in the new faith. Many residents of Medina had converted in the earlier years of the Prophet's preaching, and others became Muslim when he arrived. For those individuals and tribes that did not, the Prophet Muhammad created something that has become known as the Constitution of Medina, a pact of amity, respect for identity, and commitment to the common defense among the diverse tribes of Medina.

The escape from Mecca and the building of a Muslim community in Medina in the year 622 are considered such watershed events that the Islamic calendar begins in that year, not the year the Prophet was born, nor even the year he received his first revelation.

The implications are clear. It is a sacred duty to build a city where diverse identities are respected, where relationships are formed between communities, where promises are made to protect what is held in common. Immigrants are holy. Welcomers are holy. People who help establish "home" are holy.

It occurred to me that the Immigration Act of 1965 had passed just a year before King marched in Marquette Park. Its principal achievement was dramatically expanding immigration from around the world, which is to say, lifting the racist restrictions that had characterized American immigration policy since at least the Chinese Exclusion Act of 1882. That immigration legislation was spiritually connected to the antiracist laws advanced by the civil rights movement. Robert Kennedy said, "As we are working to remove the vestiges of racism from our public life, we cannot maintain racism as the cornerstone of our immigration policies."[3] All the Muslim immigrants from South Asia, the Middle East, West Africa, and the Pacific owed our new "home" in the United States at least in part to the African Americans who fought, bled, and died in the streets for racial restrictions to fall.

IMAN is an institution of what I call Big-Tent Citizen Islam. It is Big Tent in that it proactively welcomes Muslims from a range of backgrounds—immigrants and African Americans, urban and suburban, highly observant and not so much so. IMAN is Citizen in that its main focus is to contribute here, in the United States. It anchors this focus by emphasizing that, in the origin story of American Islam, the earliest pilgrims were not the immigrants of the mid-1960s but rather African slaves in the seventeenth century. Their survival itself is an achievement, their cultural forms are a talisman, and the "emigration" of parts of this community back to their home tradition of Islam in the mid-twentieth century, a historical period that coincides with the immigration of significant numbers of Muslims from different parts of the world, presents the United States with a massive opportunity. American Muslims are the most racially and ethnically diverse group of Muslims to ever live together in a single political entity. If the Hajj is holy in part because it serves as an opportunity to gather a stunning diversity of Muslims together in harmony and community, then the centripetal pull of this patch of land makes America sacred ground.

The current Muslim experience in America has parallels in other religious communities. American Catholicism in the first decades of the twentieth century is one analogue. In cities like Chicago, neighborhoods were defined by particular ethnic Catholic parishes—Italian Catholics here, Irish Catholics there, German Catholics farther afield. Lines did not easily cross. The common experience of anti-Catholic bigotry and the emergence of Catholic social service and civic institutions like Catholic Charities not only brought Catholics from a wide range of previously siloed ethnic and national backgrounds together but also placed them on the vanguard of Catholic institutions to be in contact with Protestants through the common cause of social service and community development.[4] These institutions and experiences created an American Catholicism.

Catholic intellectuals played a key role in helping Catholicism become an American religion. For many generations, the Catholic Church advanced the view that Catholics should seek to live in majority-Catholic nations, "confessional states." John Courtney Murray, the Jesuit scholar who was first silenced by the Church and later became a highly influential voice during the Vatican II proceedings, drew from Catholic sources and traditions as he wrote about the virtues of building a pluralist society.

American Islam has produced a Muslim version of John Courtney Murray—Dr. Umar Abd-Allah. In his highly influential paper "Islam and the Cultural Imperative," Abd-Allah writes,

> For centuries, Islamic civilization harmonized indigenous forms of cultural expression with the universal norms of its sacred law. It struck a balance between temporal beauty and ageless truth and fanned a brilliant peacock's tail of unity in diversity from the heart of China to the shores of the Atlantic. Islamic jurisprudence helped facilitate this creative genius.... Sustained cultural

relevance to distinct peoples, diverse places, and different times underlay Islam's long success as a global civilization. . . . In history, Islam showed itself to be culturally friendly and, in that regard, has been likened to a crystal clear river. Its waters (Islam) are pure, sweet, and life-giving but—having no color of their own—reflect the bedrock (indigenous culture) over which they flow. In China, Islam looked Chinese; in Mali, it looked African.[5]

In the United States, Abd-Allah once told me, Islam looked like the work of IMAN.

Rami tells the story of a woman approaching him after one of his talks about Islam and saying, "Meeting and hearing you has changed how I view Muslims. But I'm from rural Kentucky, and my people there are probably not going to get the chance to meet someone like you. What stories should I tell them about you and your Muslim community?"

Rami responded, "It's not so much the stories that you tell about me and the Muslim community that matter. It's the new story you tell about America that counts—the story you tell about all of us."

7

Postscript
Potluck Nation

There is a scene in Kumail Nanjiani's film *The Big Sick*, an autobiographical account of his dating and ultimately marrying a white woman, that highlights some of the clichés about America and its Muslims (or Muslims and their America) in this moment. Nanjiani's parents have grudgingly accepted his desire to be a stand-up comic, which Nanjiani describes in one of his routines as a professional aspiration that carries a status just below that of joining a terrorist group within his ethnoreligious community (it's a joke). But they have drawn the line at a relationship with a non-Muslim white American.

Nanjiani has been living something of a double life, dating his white girlfriend and hanging out at bars on the one hand, and on the other dutifully going to dinners at his parents' home, during which they introduce him to a steady stream of Pakistani Muslim girls in hopes of arranging a marriage. But when his girlfriend falls sick, Nanjiani decides he can't take the duality anymore. He needs his parents to know about and support his relationship.

At this point, the conversation takes a clash-of-civilizations turn.

Nanjiani's parents say, "All we wanted from you is that you be a good Muslim and marry a Pakistani girl."

Nanjiani, in an uncharacteristic moment of anger, explodes: "Why did you bring me to America if you did not want me to live as an American?"[1]

The scene is well acted, the timing of the dialogue is perfect, the pain of the characters palpable. The audience is meant to be disturbed, and on the surface, we are. But at the same time, even amid the drama, there is something strangely familiar about what we are watching. The truth is, we have seen a version of this show match a thousand times. Hero American culture, with its celebrated creativity and individuality, in this corner; the minority-religion villain of the day, with its various restrictions and old-world ways, in the opposite. As Hollywood tells it, hero America wins, the minority religion is subdued, and human evolution moves a step forward. You can almost hear the music from *Fiddler on the Roof*.

The truth about America and its minority religions, Islam included, is far more complicated and interesting. The genius of this nation is not in how it vanquishes minority religions but rather in how it welcomes their contributions. The setup is like a potluck supper. For the larger community to eat, everybody needs to bring a dish. Certain guidelines are given, but nobody is expected to follow a precise recipe. As the demographics of the population shift, so will the flavors of the food on the table. Along the way, conversation happens, palates widen, fusions emerge. There are tensions, and there is feasting.

In 2017, the Tunisian French scholar Nadia Marzouki published a book called *Islam: An American Religion*. Muslims have become American, Marzouki claims, because they are increasingly focused on contributing within the American frame—bringing their dishes to the potluck—and expanding the table along the way. She states, "It's out of the materials of *American* politics, law and culture generally that Muslims are building the norms of their discourse and their public actions. In political and legal battles, their audience and interlocutor is the American public, not some hypothetical global *ummah*."[2]

In his Netflix show *Homecoming King*, Hasan Minhaj tells a story that illustrates Marzouki's point and highlights some of the conflicts taking place along the way. The story is about a racist attack that occurs at his home in Davis, California, right after 9/11, while Hasan is in high school. As the Minhaj family receives a threatening phone call from one group of bigots, they hear loud noises coming from outside. Another group has smashed in the windows of their car. Hasan, knowing that they can't be far, runs up and down the street looking for them, blood streaming down his arm from an ill-fated attempt to reach through the broken window and retrieve his bag from the backseat of the car. He returns to the driveway to see his father stoically sweeping up the glass. The father turns to the son and says, "These things happen, and these things will continue to happen. That's the price we pay for being here."

Hasan calls this the American dream tax, which he explains is something that some immigrants and minorities simply accept. He describes it thus: you are going to endure some racism, which, if it doesn't kill you, is simply the price that must be paid for living in a nation that belongs to someone else.

That is not how Hasan understands his life in America. He has what he calls "the audacity of equality." "I'm in Honors Gov," he says, looking steely-eyed at his audience. "I have it right here: Life, liberty and the pursuit of happiness. All men are created equal. I'm equal. I don't deserve this."[3]

We live in a nation that offers those terms to all peoples. And we have a history replete with instances in which, when the terms of equality and dignity are not freely given, they have been taken. That is how people become American. That is how this nation became America.

Commentaries

8

The Challenge of Pluralism after the End of White Christian America

Robert P. Jones

Why Religious Pluralism Is So Hard

In the opening section in this book, Eboo Patel argues that, of all the forms of diversity that are most salient to our shared civic life, "religious diversity may be the one that the Founders came closest to getting right" (4). As evidence, he points to the simple but powerful dual principles in the First Amendment to the U.S. Constitution, which protect the free exercise of religion by citizens and prohibit the state from establishing or favoring one religion over another. Patel convincingly points to examples from George Washington, Thomas Jefferson, and James Madison—all of whom wrote eloquently and fiercely about religious freedom and laid a strong foundation for what was seen at the time as a bold, perhaps foolhardy, experiment.

The success of this experiment was still raising eyebrows in the late nineteenth and early twentieth centuries, when astute European observers such as Max Weber from Germany, Alexis de Tocqueville from France, and G. K. Chesterton from England—all societies with monarchies and official state churches—came to the United States to see for themselves exactly how the Americans were pulling off this unlikely feat. Each concluded, in different ways, that the key was a flourishing civil society, which formed character and fostered high levels of civic participation through voluntary organizations, not least of which was a dizzying array of churches and other religious organizations.

Despite this strong foundation and two centuries of relative success navigating this complex terrain, our contemporary situation presents some unprecedented challenges. No American generation before the current one has fully faced a test of our commitment to the free exercise of religion. For the first one hundred years of the republic, white Anglo-Saxon Protestants were such a dominant cultural force and demographic reality that the practical impact of the establishment and growth of other religious groups was negligible. They posed a threat neither to the cultural fabric nor to political power.

But with a strong uptick in immigration from Ireland, the Mediterranean, and eastern Europe in the late nineteenth and early twentieth centuries, with high numbers of Catholic and Jewish immigrants, the white Protestant establishment began to actively guard its turf. The requests of Jews and Catholics to be admitted inside the gates of acceptable American civil religion were met with strong opposition and violence. The Know-Nothing Party, the KKK, and other white Protestant supremacist groups targeted not just black Americans but also Jews and Catholics as groups that could never be, properly speaking, "white" or "American." Through the tumultuous decades marked by two world wars and the Great Depression, notions of whiteness slowly expanded to admit Jewish, Italian, and Irish immigrants, and the term *Judeo-Christian* began to be employed as an umbrella term for the core religious American culture. By the 1950s, as documented in Will Herberg's classic book *Protestant, Catholic, Jew*, the country was at least beginning to accept the idea of a "triple melting pot."[1]

These past lessons and achievements, however, are only partially instructive for our more complicated present, for at least two reasons. First, even a cursory glance at the achievements of religious pluralism in America reveals that the acceptance of religious diversity has always been entangled with perceptions of race. In the past, the American solution has been to finesse the issue of race by broadening the definition of whiteness, rather than to deal with the problem of racism head on. But Patel's test case of Muslim integration into the American religious fabric shows the difficulty of dusting off this strategy for the present. In America, while the historical elasticity of whiteness clearly reveals it to be a social construct, it remains at least partially connected to lighter skin tone. Full acceptance of dark-skinned Muslim Americans, African Americans, or the diverse groups who have immigrated from South Asia, Africa, and the Middle East—using this strategy—seems highly unlikely.

Second, virtually every previous strategy for accepting religious diversity relied on the melting pot idea. In the great American stew, cultural and even ethnic differences literally dissolved and evaporated, leaving a reduction that was palatable to white Protestant tastes. Assimilation was the expectation. And while the question was almost always left implicit, the unstated assumption was that newer religious groups, to be fully accepted, should conform to a white Protestant ideal. Jewish immigrants, for example, rapidly learned English; prominently displayed American flags in their synagogues, which often followed Christian architectural forms; and formed themselves into denominations. But this melting pot strategy also depended on the existence of a strong reference group that provided the model and sat in the seat of cultural power—something we lack today. And as I explain later, that world of white Protestantism, and even the broader world of white Christendom, has passed from the scene in the last generation.[2]

If we're going to chart a course for a new kind of religious diversity, we'll have to move beyond the tread-worn strategies of finessing racial identity and melting pot conformity.

America's Struggle with Pluralism:
More about Displacement than Diversity

THE CURRENT RELIGIOUS LANDSCAPE

Since the 1990s, the U.S. religious landscape has experienced an enormous amount of change. The most outstanding features are the precipitous decline of white, non-Hispanic Christian groups and a correspondingly strong rise of religiously unaffiliated Americans. Trends also show steady growth among Latino Christian groups and stability among African American Christians. There has also been modest growth among non-Christian religious groups—such as Jews, Muslims, Buddhists, and Hindus—although these groups combined are still in single digits as a percentage of the general population.

Given the cultural and demographic dominance of white Christians, and especially white Protestants, in the nation's history, their steep decline over the last three decades is nothing short of astonishing. The year 1993 was the last in which white Protestants constituted a majority (51 percent) of the public. Today, white Protestants account for only 30 percent of Americans. Most notably, if one considers all white Christian groups combined—Protestant, Catholic, and nondenominational—we have just recently crossed a significant milestone: over the last decade, demographically speaking, the country has shifted from a majority white Christian country to a minority white Christian country—from 54 percent in 2008 to 43 percent in 2016, a drop of 11 percentage points.[3]

The ranks of the religiously unaffiliated have swelled during this same period. As recently as the mid-1990s, the percentage of religiously unaffiliated Americans—those who say they are atheist, agnostic, or nothing in particular in response to a religious identification question—was still in single digits. In 1994, only 9 percent of Americans identified as religiously unaffiliated, but that number nearly tripled to 24 percent by 2016.[4]

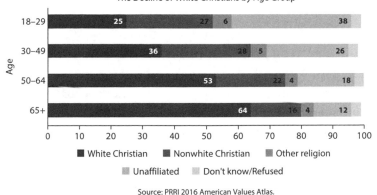

The Decline of White Christians by Age Group

Source: PRRI 2016 American Values Atlas.

As the figure above shows, examining the gaps in patterns of religious affiliation between the generations that are alive today illustrates just how quickly these transformations have happened. Nearly two-thirds (64 percent) of seniors (ages sixty-five and older) identify as white and Christian, compared to only about one-quarter (25 percent) of young Americans under the age of thirty. Conversely, more than three times as many young Americans as seniors identify as religiously unaffiliated (38 percent versus 12 percent, respectively).

Today, non-Christian religious groups constitute 6 percent of all Americans, up modestly from 5 percent in the mid-1990s.[5] Jews constitute 2 percent of the public, while Muslims, Hindus, and Buddhists each constitute 1 percent; all other non-Christian religions combined constitute another 1 percent of Americans. This slight growth is also reflected in generational differences: only 4 percent of seniors, compared to 6 percent of younger Americans, identify with a non-Christian religion.

THE ENGINES TRANSFORMING
THE AMERICAN RELIGIOUS LANDSCAPE

When I talk about these engines, I typically talk about "the three Ds": demographic change, declining birth rates, and disaffiliation.

At least part of the decline of white Christians in America is due to demographic change, primarily driven by increased Hispanic immigration, largely from Mexico. Since about two-thirds of Mexican immigrants are Catholic, these dynamics have particularly impacted the Catholic Church. In the early 1990s, for example, the ratio of white to nonwhite Catholics was approximately ten to one. But by 2016, those numbers were approaching parity nationwide, and in the West, Hispanic Catholics now outnumber white Catholics.[6] The rising number of Hispanic Americans is also shifting the balance in the evangelical Protestant world, where the proportion of Hispanic Protestants—mostly Pentecostal and charismatic—is increasing, while the proportion of white, non-Hispanic evangelicals is shrinking.

Declining birth rates among white Americans are also a frequently overlooked source of change in the American religious marketplace.[7] As a result, the median age of white Christians has been creeping up over the last few decades. The median age of white evangelical Protestants and white Catholics is fifty-five, slightly higher than that of white mainline Protestants, which is fifty-four. Four decades earlier, the median age of these white Christian groups was much lower. In 1976, the median age of white Catholics was just forty, while the median age of white Protestants was forty-five.[8] The median age of Hindus (thirty-two), Muslims (thirty-two), Buddhists (thirty-six), religiously unaffiliated Americans (thirty-seven), and Hispanic Protestants (thirty-seven) is below forty.[9]

As noted earlier, the growing number of religiously unaffiliated Americans, especially among young adults, is also fueling changes in the religious landscape. One objection to the significance of this factor is that younger Americans are always less religiously affiliated than older Americans. Once these carefree twenty-somethings get married and have kids, the argument goes, they'll return to churches later in life. In other words, the argument is that what we're seeing is a life-cycle effect of being in one's twenties, rather than a generational effect that will remain with this cohort as they age.

However, there are at least three reasons why we should expect this generation to continue to be the most religiously unaffiliated generation the country has ever known. First, young Americans (ages eighteen to twenty-nine) today are approximately three times as unaffiliated as Baby Boomers were in their twenties (38 percent versus 13 percent).[10] So even if the same proportion of younger Americans were to affiliate in their thirties, this generation would still be significantly more unaffiliated than any other in history. Second, one of the biggest drivers for religiously unaffiliated adults to reaffiliate is having a religious spouse who pulls the other partner back toward the institution, but today, there is evidence that religiously unaffiliated people are increasingly seeking each other out as marriage partners.[11]

Third, there is evidence that many young people have disaffiliated from religion because of political reasons, particularly over opposition to LGBT rights by conservative Christian churches. In their landmark 2010 study of the changing religious landscape, *American Grace*, sociologists Robert Putnam and David Campbell sum up the conflict this way: "This group of young people came of age when 'religion' was identified publicly with the Religious Right, and exactly at the time when the leaders of that movement put homosexuality and gay marriage at the top of their agenda. And yet this is the very generation in which the new tolerance of homosexuality has grown most rapidly. In short, just as the younger cohort of Americans was zigging in one direction, many highly visible religious leaders zagged in the other."[12]

Overall, then, we expect to see the major transformations in the American religious landscape continue, at least into the near future.

THE REAL CHALLENGE FOR RELIGIOUS PLURALISM IN AMERICA

Looking at the numbers, especially the relatively modest numbers of non-Christian, religiously affiliated Americans, it may seem a bit puzzling that integrating a group of religious minorities that,

combined, constitute only 6 percent of the public—only 4 percent
if we consider Jews already accepted—is such a challenge for the
country today. To take Patel's test case of Muslims, America's
1 percent Muslim population is significantly lower than France's
8.8 percent, the United Kingdom's 6.3 percent, or Germany's 6.1
percent.[13] And while the Muslim population is growing in the U.S.,
its growth rate is about one-third of the growth rate in Europe.
It will likely be 2050 before Muslim Americans overtake Jewish
Americans as the largest non-Christian religious group.[14]

This analysis points to a critical insight for the challenge of religious diversity in America. Today anxieties and resistance stem not
primarily from increasing *diversity* but rather from a sense of *displacement* among significant numbers of white Christians as they
realize they no longer enjoy majority status.

A range of survey questions asked ahead of the 2016 election
by the Public Religion Research Institute (PRRI) and the *Atlantic*
captured this anxiety about external threats and internal displacement among whites overall and white Christians in particular. Solid
majorities of white evangelical Protestants (81 percent), white mainline Protestants (65 percent), and white Catholics (62 percent), for
example, agree that "the American way of life needs to be protected
from foreign influence," compared to 55 percent of all Americans.
White evangelical Protestants are particularly anxious: majorities
agree both that "today, America is in danger of losing its culture and
identity" (76 percent) and that "things have changed so much that
I often feel like a stranger in my own country" (51 percent). These
last sentiments played a particularly powerful role in the 2016 election.
Aside from political partisanship, agreeing with these sentiments
was the strongest single nondemographic independent predictor of
support for Donald Trump's presidency for both white evangelical
Protestants and white working-class Americans.[15]

White Christian displacement as America's undisputed dominant group is significant for two reasons. First, it undermines a core

American strategy for dealing with religious diversity: expecting conformity toward a strong majority group. Second, and perhaps more importantly, many white Christian groups have experienced these declines as an existential threat, fueling visceral emotions such as anxiety, alarm, and anger. The resulting mentality among white Christians of hunkered-down defensiveness, rather than open-handed generosity, may be the biggest barrier to dealing with the challenges of religious and ethnic diversity that lie before us today. It is less a practical problem than a problem of civic, or even theological, imagination and faith.

Partisan Erosion of a Shared Sense of American Identity

Full clarity about the scale of the challenges to religious pluralism has been hindered by academic siloes dividing religious studies, sociology, and political science. Those who are focused on interfaith relations and dialogue, anchored in religious studies and sociology, have often neglected the role that increasing partisanship is playing in shaping Americans' responses to religious diversity. And political scientists working to document the sharp rise in partisanship have not, for the most part, made religious diversity concerns a central research problem. But making these connections, especially in the wake of the brutal 2016 presidential campaign, in which American identity was the primary election issue, is vital.

Recent survey data provides troubling evidence that amid the shockwaves from these demographic and religious transformations, our two political parties are reorienting themselves away from the more familiar liberal versus conservative alignment and toward new poles of cultural pluralism versus monism. In other words, like so many other issues in American public life, religious pluralism has now been prominently installed as a totem, marking partisan tribal territory.

Over the last fifty years, our two political parties have been sorting themselves into different factions, largely over reactions to civil rights and related issues of racial, ethnic, and religious diversity. As the Democratic Party became associated with the civil rights movement, following the Johnson administration's passage of landmark legislation like the Civil Rights Act (1964) and the Voting Rights Act (1965), large numbers of disgruntled whites in the South began to defect to the Republican Party. In the 1964 election, for the first time since the Civil War, more southern whites voted for the Republican candidate than for the Democrat, setting a precedent that has held true for every subsequent presidential election. By the time of Ronald Reagan's presidency, "the great white switch" had solidified, and southern whites have remained staunch Republicans.[16]

As these dynamics have played out, they have resulted in our two political parties having wildly divergent makeups.[17] In a massive survey of over one hundred thousand Americans, PRRI's American Values Atlas found that only 29 percent of Democrats, for example, identify as white and Christian, compared to nearly three-quarters (73 percent) of Republicans. Democrats are about three times as likely as Republicans to report being affiliated with a non-Christian religion (5 percent versus 2 percent, respectively); PRRI found virtually no Muslims, Hindus, or Buddhists among self-identified Republicans. Finally, religious and nonreligious Americans are sorting themselves along partisan lines as well: more than one-quarter (26 percent) of Democrats, compared to only 11 percent of Republicans, are religiously unaffiliated.[18]

Given this sorting, the nearly mirror-opposite partisan reactions to the question of what kind of culture is important for American identity become more understandable. A recent Associated Press–NORC poll found that approximately two-thirds (66 percent) of Democrats, compared with only 35 percent of Republicans, said the mixing of cultures and values from around the world was extremely or very important to American identity. Conversely, nearly two-thirds of Republicans (64 percent), compared with 32 percent of Democrats, saw a culture grounded in Christian religious beliefs as extremely or very important to American identity.[19]

These divergent orientations can also be seen in a 2017 PRRI poll that explored partisan perceptions of which groups are facing discrimination in the country today. Like Americans overall, large majorities of Democrats believe that minority groups such as African Americans, immigrants, and Muslims face a lot of discrimination in the country. Only about one in five Democrats says that majority groups such as Christians or whites face a lot of discrimination in the U.S. today. Republicans, on the other hand, are much less likely than Democrats to believe any minority group faces a lot of discrimination, and they believe that Christians and whites face roughly as much discrimination as immigrants and Muslims. Notably, Republicans believe that African Americans are significantly less likely than whites or Christians to experience a lot of discrimination (27 percent versus 43 percent and 48 percent, respectively).[20]

Taken as a whole, these partisan portraits highlight contrasting responses to the country's changing demographics and culture. Democrats are embracing these changes as central to their vision of an evolving American identity that is strengthened and renewed by diversity. By contrast, Republicans see these changes eroding a core white Christian American identity and perceive themselves to be under siege as the country changes around them.

The fabric of American identity has been stretched in similar ways before—for example, the Civil War, reactions to heightened immigration at the turn of the twentieth century, and the cultural upheavals of the 1960s. But in each of these crises, white Christians—whatever their fears—still served as a secure demographic and cultural majority in the nation.

Americans from both political parties sense the unraveling of a broadly shared consensus about American identity. About seven in ten Republicans and Democrats fear that the United States is losing its national identity, compared with only three in ten who say it is secure, per the AP-NORC survey. The two political parties may not share much, but each is increasingly aware that the other has embraced a radically different vision of America's identity and future.

One of the biggest obstacles to progress in the area of religious pluralism is the way that diversity has been weaponized in partisan politics. The temptation for the Republican Party is to double down on a form of white Christian nationalism, which treats racial and religious identity as tribal markers and defends a shrinking demographic with increasingly autocratic assertions of power. The Democratic Party is contending with the challenges of organizing its more diverse coalition and is also facing its own tribal temptations to embrace an identity politics that has room to celebrate every group *except* whites who strongly identify as Christian. If this realignment continues unabated, left out of this binary opposition will be a not insignificant number of whites who are both wary of white Christian nationalism and weary of feeling discounted in the marketplace of identity politics. And our great national motto will have devolved from a praiseworthy *E pluribus unum* to a paranoid *E pluribus duo*.

These responses to demographic and cultural change, carried along by the currents of a presidential campaign that foregrounded these issues like none in recent memory, are shifting the magnetic field that defines the two parties.

The Challenge of Our Day

In my family's dining room is an antique table from the 1940s with six chairs. But one of the chairs is constructed differently from the rest. It is broader than the other chairs, and it is the only one with armrests. Sometimes called "the captain's chair," it was designed for the head of the table. Historically, that chair was meant to architecturally reinforce hierarchical family relationships, with the father occupying that throne-like seat, from which he could control the flow of the meal and the topics of conversation.[21]

If we imagine America gathered around a dining-room table, until very recently, white Christians, and particularly white Protestants, felt like they owned the table and were entitled to the patriarch's position. Others might be invited to pull up a chair, either as subordinate family members or as guests, but the power relationships and expectations were understood by all. If we are going to make progress toward fulfilling our nation's promise of religious liberty for all, we have to be clear about the problem. The chief impediment for pluralism today is not that we have run out of chairs. Rather, it is that many white Christians have been reluctant to relinquish the privileged seat of power.

Even though the contemporary problems we are facing are historically unique, I agree with Patel that returning to the early European observers of American democracy may still yield insights. While Tocqueville and Weber have much to teach us, the less known, prolific British writer and social commentator G. K. Chesterton may be more instructive in our current cultural moment. Chesterton focuses less than Tocqueville and Weber on the role of religious voluntary organizations and more on how the founding documents, and the founding ideals they contained, structured American identity in a way that did not depend on shared religion or race.

After Chesterton visited the United States for the first time in 1921, he was so fascinated by the distinctiveness of the country that he published his reflections in a book titled *What I Saw in America*.[22] In that account, he famously concluded that America was "a nation with the soul of a church." He clarified what he meant with this intriguing turn of phrase: "America is the only nation in the world that is founded on a creed. That creed is set forth with dogmatic and even theological lucidity in the Declaration of Independence. . . . It enunciates that all men are equal in their claim to justice, that governments exist to give them that justice, and that their authority is for that reason just."[23]

Chesterton's metaphorical language is often misunderstood. As this extended quote makes clear, Chesterton was referring not to the nation's religiosity but rather to its formation around a set of core *political* beliefs—a civic "creed"—enshrined in founding "sacred texts" such as the Declaration of Independence and the Constitution. Chesterton was intrigued by the fact that the United States, unlike European nations, did not rely on ethnic kinship, cultural character, an official state religion, or a "national type" for a shared identity. The profoundness of the American experiment, he argued, was that it aspired to create "a home out of vagabonds and a nation out of exiles," who would be united principally by voluntary assent to creedal *political* beliefs such as the equality of all people.

To be sure, Chesterton underestimated the distance between these lofty principles and the confounding realities. The United States has always struggled to live up to the ideals enshrined in our founding documents, as prophets such as the Rev. Dr. Martin Luther King Jr. and others have reminded us. But Chesterton's instinct to ground a shared cultural worldview not in common ethnic or religious identity but rather in shared political commitments may prove fertile ground for the present.

The key, I think, is to move away from models that require greater conformity and thicker agreement at the cultural level. Take, for example, the ideas of the melting pot and widely shared civil religion, which fit hand in glove. Groups are expected to conform to white Anglo-Saxon Protestant cultural norms and to become fluent in the theistic language of American civil religion. But at this stage in our nation's history, thick models such as these ask too much of religious minority groups and the religiously unaffiliated at the same time that they chafe as too thin for many white Christians.

For religious minority groups and religiously unaffiliated Americans, the decentering of a single religio-racial majority undermines melting pot solutions in at least two ways. First, the absence of a clear target culture to serve as an assimilation telos makes this demand, if not nonsensical, at least confusing. Second, the retreat of a single dominant culture means there is no longer a dispenser of rewards and punishments for assimilation. White Christians have lost their big stick and are reaching into the bottom of their bag of carrots. With fewer and fewer goods exclusively reserved to be granted from white Christians in power, religious minority groups are finding that the sacrifices assimilation often involves are no longer worth it.

The main reason that the civil religion project has run aground since its heyday in the 1970s and 1980s is not that the country has become full of nontheists who cannot affirm its basic tenets—even a majority (59 percent) of the religiously unaffiliated affirm a belief in God.[24] A clue to the depth of the problem is that the civil religion consensus, with its boundary set at a generic theism, has come under attack most strongly in the last decade from the right, from conservative white Christians.

What explains this shift from the 1980s, when President Reagan and Billy Graham were happily espousing versions of American civil religion that seemed to seamlessly coexist with Christianity? Simply put, the end of the era of white Christian America changed the valence of civil religion for white Christians. From the secure standpoint of cultural and demographic dominance, the idea of a civil religion was a generous concession to other citizens, all of whom were expected to understand its true source. But on the other side of cultural decentering and the demographic decline of a white Protestant majority, the generic theism of civil religion now has to be seriously faced on its own terms. In this new environment, the idea of civil religion feels less like a reinforcement of Christian values and more like a threat to white Protestant particularity. Returning to Chesterton's observations may provide a way beyond the civil religion dilemma.

It is notable that Chesterton's conclusion about the forces that created a unique American character and rich social solidarity did not include the dominance of white Protestant religious institutions, as Tocqueville's account did, or the Protestant work ethic, as

Weber's account did. Rather, what struck him was the way in which a strong commitment to the ideals of a democratic society created bonds of solidarity that held together a motley, diverse group of people. Their claims to be a part of the nation were dependent only on the strength of their commitment to the democratic creeds found in the sacred texts of the nation's founding documents.

Chesterton's civic creedalism is generally consistent with the vision Patel lays out, and its recovery helps address some of the areas where Patel's proposal may run into difficulty. First, it is consistent with the example Patel cites of President Washington's letter to the early Jewish community in the country, in which he assures them that the U.S. government stands for equal liberty of, not just toleration for, religious minorities. Washington responds to these early Jewish Americans with a straightforward statement of civil principles: "For happily the government of the United States, which gives to bigotry no sanction, to persecution no assistance, requires only that they who live under its protection, should demean themselves as good citizens" (5).

Second, a civic creedalism would resonate more deeply with America's burgeoning group of religiously unaffiliated Americans, who at 24 percent of the country already exceed the size of the largest religious groups in the country. While about six in ten hold some belief in God and roughly half (47 percent) say they retain a connection to religion as part of their ethnic background or cultural heritage, religiously unaffiliated Americans are also highly skeptical of religious organizations. Nearly two-thirds (66 percent), for example, say that religion causes more problems in society than it solves.[25] Rather than forcing religiously unaffiliated Americans to wrestle with these complicated views about religion, which may have a somewhat alienating effect, a civic creedalism levels the playing field and asks religiously unaffiliated and affiliated Americans for the same affirmations.

Third, a civic creedalism may provide a solution to two problems that Patel identifies with the civil religion solution. The first problem is that American civil religion historically was drawn explicitly from Protestant Christianity, which was then later expanded to include more broadly "the Judeo-Christian tradition, specifically the Old and New Testaments" (25). This symbolic improvisation has proved useful in the country's past, as its regular use by leaders as diverse as Lincoln, King, and Reagan testifies. While Patel rightly objects to the exclusionary "limiting of our civil religious tradition to symbols and vocabularies drawn from two religions," he argues that there may be enough symbolic elasticity in American civil religion to retain it while incorporating other sacred texts and religious vocabularies (25).

I would argue, however, that the creative invention of *Judeo-Christian* represents the outer boundary for the civil religion tradition. Even with these closely related religious traditions, the term has been awkward, especially for those on the minority side of the hyphen. It has been stretched and finessed to the breaking point, and it is time to let it go. Rather than attempting to add another hyphen— "the Judeo-Christian-Muslim-unaffiliated tradition" doesn't exactly trip off the tongue—it is time to rethink its basis, which was always, at its root, white Anglo-Saxon Protestantism. That basis has never been clearer than it is today, in the twilight of white Christian dominance. In this light, the wisdom of a civic creedalism seems all the more promising, as the foundation rests on affirmations all Americans can make in their own first languages, and none are asked to translate more than others.

The second problem a civic creedalism might solve is that it lowers the conflict for religious communities between the universal and particular. Extending a line from political philosopher Michael Walzer, Patel notes, "If the challenge of the diverse society is to embrace its differences and maintain a common life, the challenge of the particular religious community is to embrace the nation's common life while maintaining its difference" (27). Patel goes on to argue that it is in our compelling interest for religious groups to be able to "harmonize their distinctive traditions with national ideals" (15).

I certainly agree that particular traditions need to be able to connect with basic American ideals and the idea of the common good. But the civil religion tradition is problematic here.

The musical metaphor is an apt one to illustrate the difficulties. For example, Eastern music sounds exotic to many Western ears because it uses a "double harmonic," or "Arabic," scale. There are quartertones in this scale that don't even exist in Western music. If the dominant melody of civil religion is Protestant Christianity composed within the bounds of a Western scale, it may not be so simple to suggest that religious minorities or the religiously unaffiliated simply "harmonize" with it. The cultural notes just may not exist. The civic creedalism tradition, however, demands less. It might be thought of less as a melody than as a tempo or time signature that allows for more freedom of expression. And it may not demand that everyone play at once. There are times for orchestral cooperation, and there are times for breathtaking solos that add to the whole but that would never find expression under the constraints of a Western scale.

Finally, a civic creedalism provides rich enough soil to inspire the "poetry and poetics" of civil discourse without being overly prescriptive of the form. This is fitting for the Americans, who are also generally a practical people. Americans break out their civic and rhetorical toolkits not in the abstract but in response to particular moral and political problems. Social theory should pay more attention to the messiness—and creativity—of what these conversations look like on the ground. In his influential book *Ethics after Babel*, religious studies scholar Jeffrey Stout argued that "the creative intellectual task . . . of every generation involves moral bricolage,"[26] the project of stitching together varieties of moral and religious discourse and practice into justifications for principles and solutions for contemporary problems. Citizens and political leaders create their discourse on the fly, with pragmatic concerns about audience, effectiveness, appropriateness, and other criteria that are specific to the situation at hand.

This may sound like fairly thin gruel to nurture democracy. But it is more than it seems. As social scientist Steven Tipton argues, while we may no longer have a consensus around a thick civil religion, what holds us together is "the coherence of our moral disagreement and argument within an ongoing cultural conversation that embraces multiple moral traditions, languages, and practices in the interrelation of their social settings."[27] And as Tipton notes, these arguments and tensions are not only between different groups of citizens but also to some degree within each of us in a pluralistic society as we embody different identities across varied institutional homes.

All in all, a civic creedalism may provide the most nourishing soil for the survival of a healthy democracy, where diverse religious and cultural groups—and even we within ourselves—are engaged in a historically extended, moral argument about the common good. It may be contentious, and it may seem thin compared to conversations that might take place among more homogeneous communities; but if it remains coherent and grounded in at least some shared touchstones, it may be enough.

Conclusion

American pluralism is at a crossroads—a place, as Patel describes it, where "we discover that our civil religion narrative no longer connects our past with our present and with our hoped-for future in a satisfactory way" (24). I have argued that our current moment demands that we rethink our path. We can be grateful for our forebears, who worked creatively to hitch other train cars to the engine of white Protestantism, so that Jews and Catholics and Protestants of color could be included on the journey. But as we look at the challenges ahead—an increasingly diverse religious landscape without a white Christian majority, coupled with strong partisan divides—we find that exhausted engine is no longer capable of carrying the load into the future.

One of Patel's best insights is the proposition that "in American civil religion we do not deify a position so much as we sacralize a discourse" (28). Here, he is pointing to the dynamic cultural potential to remake our national narrative over time. This is certainly right. But Patel mistakes the cultural creativity of which civil religion is a part for civil religion itself. Civil religion is not the necessary vehicle for a poetic or sacred discourse about American ideals. By my lights, an approach grounded in civic creedalism has more to offer this project at this point in our history, primarily because its lower affirmational demands open up more inclusive space for creative solutions that were unimaginable under the constraints of civil religion thinking.

By reaching for less threshold agreement, we open up more space for conversation. Under these conditions, the project Patel shows that we need seems more likely to flourish: "So we listen to new voices, we add some symbols and deemphasize others, elevate these stories and demote those, and reinterpret the whole narrative so that we continue being America, or rather, become a better America" (24). Such a model will sound much less like a harmonized chorus and much more like an extended cultural argument. To many civic-minded Republicans who worry about social cohesion, that may sound insufficient. But if the argument is lively, engaged, and coherent, it may prove that a return to our founding civic creedalism is enough, after all, to create one out of many.

9

Hope without a Common Good

John Inazu

y friend and colleague Eboo Patel has ably situated some of the challenges and opportunities of living together in a society with deep differences. In many ways, Patel's descriptions and aspirations echo those that I have offered in my recent book, *Confident Pluralism: Surviving and Thriving through Deep Difference.*[1] But I believe Patel's essay departs from my arguments in two related ways. First, he is too optimistic about what we as citizens of this country hold in common with one another. Second, he neglects the current shortcomings of the legal protections that we need in order to live together in spite of our differences.

The reader will detect an oddity in these two friendly challenges to Patel's argument. On one hand, I suggest that we may not have the unity that Patel imagines. On the other hand, I argue that we need to strengthen the legal protections that allow our differences to remain. So in the face of less unity, I argue for reinforcing our differences. In one sense, this tension points to the tragic dimension of politics: despite our yearnings for peace and unity, those elusive goals inevitably escape us in this life. But there is at least a partial resolution to the paradox: we must find enough of a modest unity to agree that we need to protect our differences. Authentic relationships across differences recognize rather than ignore the limits to our unity. As I will suggest toward the end of my response, the challenge to find this modest unity is nowhere more pressing than when it comes to the American Muslim experience out of which Patel writes. But first, let me turn to Patel's optimism.

Patel's Optimism for America

Although I agree with much of Patel's vision for our country, some of his appeals strike me as overly optimistic. That critique is not without some irony coming from me—commentators have suggested that *Confident Pluralism* offers "little hope" (Rod Dreher),[2] that it arrives "too late" (Paul Horwitz),[3] and that it is "[doomed] to immediate irrelevance" (Carl Trueman).[4] But from one optimist to another, let me suggest that Patel's reliance on a generic "civil religion" to bind us together is especially problematic.

Patel contends that America's self-understanding as a Judeo-Christian nation might grow to include other communities (8). He rightly questions the historical veracity of the term *Judeo-Christian*, but he suggests that its "genius" is that it "expands the national narrative in a manner that dignifies previously marginalized occupants" (70). There is, however, a more pragmatic and less noble history behind the term. As historian Gene Zubovich notes, evangelical Protestants initially resisted the move toward religious pluralism.[5] In 1955, Will Herberg's *Protestant, Catholic, Jew* argued for embracing interfaith cooperation between these three religions.[6] But in 1947, and again in 1954, the National Association of Evangelicals lobbied Congress for a "Christian amendment" to the Constitution that read, "This nation devoutly recognizes the authority and law of Jesus Christ, Savior and Ruler of all nations, through whom are bestowed the blessings of Almighty God."[7] Zubovich suggests that it was only in the 1960s that evangelicals started to embrace the "Judeo-Christian" label, when liberal Protestants moved toward a broader religious pluralism and, in some cases, secularism: "At the moment when liberal Protestants and others left Judeo-Christianity behind, fearing the tri-faith model was too narrow to capture the world's diversity, evangelical Protestants seized on the idea," in part because they saw "Catholics and Jews as important allies in the fight against abortion, feminism and gay rights."[8]

Apart from its dubious origins, the category of Judeo-Christianity obscures the particularity of religious traditions in a way that risks promoting a civil religion ultimately beholden to the state. I worry that Patel fails to see this risk. Following Robert Bellah, he suggests that the Judeo-Christian narrative contributes to an American tradition of civil religion that "stands separate from people's traditional faiths but draws freely from religious language to sacralize national symbols" (23).

I see why Patel and Bellah want to harness the unifying potential of a civil religious tradition. Interfaith partnerships can help to find common ground across different religions—for example, bringing together different religious groups in the common cause of religious liberty. But religious believers rooted in particular traditions may find it difficult to unite in broader and more nebulous categories like "Judeo-Christianity," to say nothing of "religion." The phrase Judeo-Christian also poses a linguistic challenge to absorbing faiths like Islam—or Hinduism, or Buddhism—into the existing narrative.

The hurdles to maintaining a generic category of religious belief increase when we consider the growing number of nonbelievers in this country. Recent polls suggest a steadily increasing segment of the population that rejects any belief in God.[9] Nonbelievers may find little appeal in an argument for "civil religion," particularly one that is rooted in a "Judeo-Christian" tradition. In fact, the divisions between Americans who hold some form of religious belief and those who identify as nonbelievers may soon dwarf whatever differences separate religious believers from one another.

Take the example of legislative prayer, highlighted in the Supreme Court's 2014 decision in Town of Greece v. Galloway.[10] The case involved a practice of the town board of the city of Greece, New York. Following roll call and the recitation of the Pledge of Allegiance, a local clergy member who was designated as the "chaplain of the month" delivered an invocation.[11] The town board selected clergy from "congregations listed in a local directory" and "at no point excluded or denied an opportunity to a would-be prayer giver."[12]

The Supreme Court upheld the practice as constitutionally permissible under the First Amendment's Establishment Clause, noting that the town's policy meant that "a minister or layperson of any persuasion, including an atheist, could give the invocation."[13] But this kind of reasoning elevates form over substance. As the Court noted, "Nearly all of the congregations in town were Christian; and from 1999 to 2007, all of the participating ministers were too."[14]

The town board's practice also affected citizens coming before the board on town business. As the majority opinion observed, "Some of the ministers spoke in a distinctly Christian idiom; and a minority invoked religious holidays, scripture, or doctrine."[15] Justice Elena Kagan illustrated the implications of these prayers in her dissent, offering a thought experiment that drew from the record before the Court:

> You are a party in a case going to trial; let's say you have filed suit against the government for violating one of your legal rights. The judge bangs his gavel to call the court to order, asks a minister to come to the front of the room, and instructs the 10 or so individuals present to rise for an opening prayer. The clergyman faces those in attendance and says: "Lord, God of all creation, . . . we acknowledge the saving sacrifice of Jesus Christ on the cross. We draw strength . . . from his resurrection at Easter. Jesus Christ, who took away the sins of the world, destroyed our death, through his dying and in his rising, he has restored our life. Blessed are you, who have raised up the Lord Jesus, you who will raise us, in our turn, and put us by His side. . . . Amen." The judge then asks your lawyer to begin the trial.[16]

Kagan suggested that by allowing this kind of prayer to open the meeting, the town board "has aligned itself with, and placed its imprimatur on, a particular religious creed." Indeed, the Court's decision ignores the social realities that now complicate officially sanctioned prayers in ways different from past eras. As Kagan observed, these prayers "express beliefs that are fundamental to some, foreign to others—and because that is so they carry the ever-present potential to both exclude and divide."[17]

As the number of Americans who see themselves as being outside any religious tradition continues to grow, the civil religious tradition will reencounter a host of practical problems that have largely been assumed away in earlier times: "nonsectarian" prayers, "In God We Trust" on our currency, "under God" in the Pledge of Allegiance, and the presence of taxpayer-funded clergy in the military, on prison staffs, and in Congress. All of these examples hail from the establishment side of religious liberty, but long-standing free-exercise norms will also encounter growing challenges. The claim that religious belief is a special kind of belief warranting special exemptions or accommodations may appeal to adherents of different religions, but it will likely be met with skepticism from those without transcendent religious commitments.[18] If an employer, a school, or the federal government accommodates a religious believer's observance of a holy day, then should it not also accommodate the nonbeliever whose most important day of the year is an anniversary, a birthday, or the Super Bowl?[19] Collapsing the distinction between religious holy days and other important days will lead quickly to either an unworkable system of individualized accommodations or a generic policy that grants everyone a set number of absences. But the alternative of maintaining the distinction between religious and nonreligious justifications may start to look like unjustly favoring religion in the eyes of the nonbeliever.

The stakes seem high enough when it comes to time off from work or an extension on a homework assignment. They run even higher when religious claimants seek exemptions from generally applicable laws and regulations like those requiring employers to provide contraceptive coverage or demanding that schools grant transgender students access to their restroom of choice. Some religious believers will see these requirements as impositions on their religious beliefs and practices. Other religious believers who don't share these particular commitments may nonetheless support the broader principle of religious liberty, knowing that their own commitments may one day be at odds with majoritarian norms. But nonbelievers may see little reason to support religious exemptions to generally applicable laws that do not offer them any tangible benefits.

None of this is meant to suggest that nonbelievers are either less principled or more rational than believers. Patel rightly notes that John Rawls viewed religious traditions as "comprehensive doctrines" (16), a term that Rawls used to describe systems of belief that address the "big questions" that people encounter during the course of their lives.[20] But Rawls also included *nonreligious* belief systems in his definition of comprehensive doctrines.[21] And it doesn't take a religious comprehensive doctrine to convince people that they are pursuing "ultimate concerns" (to borrow the phrase that Patel borrows from Paul Tillich to suggest the special potency of religious belief) (16). The impassioned citizens I witnessed on both sides of the political aisle in the 2016 presidential election often possessed a religious-like zeal, regardless of whether they rooted their allegiances in religious faith.

Nor are secularized political modes of argument any more self-evidently "rational" than religious ones. Rawls introduced the constraint of "public reason" to suggest that citizens should have coherent explanations for their voting and policy preferences, and he intimated that these explanations should be readily understandable to fellow citizens.[22] But the idea that the average "secular" voter could approach this Rawlsian standard any better than the average religious voter has always been a fiction.[23] Some philosophers and theologians may be able to articulate a justification for their views that satisfies the standards of Rawls's public reason, but the average citizen cannot explain, for example, the philosophical or jurisprudential basis for the Supreme Court's recognition of a right to abortion. Nonreligious voters, like religious voters, bring a hodgepodge of personal beliefs with them into the ballot box. And in both cases, these personal beliefs too often rely on emotional appeal and assumptions molded in echo chambers.

Patel is aware of these challenges. Like me, he wants to envision a modest unity that reaches across religious and political divides.[24] That effort is not only commendable—it is essential. We must find something that holds us together in spite of our differences. But Patel's admirable search for a modest unity leads him to Bellah's notion of civil religion and the suggestion that we should "sacralize national symbols." Law professor Paul Kahn has identified the logical end of this pursuit: "The state's territory becomes consecrated ground, its history a sacred duty to maintain, its flag something to die for. None of this has much to do with the secular; these are matters of faith, not reason."[25] Kahn's projection may be unavoidable—it might be that embracing national allegiance as a matter of faith is the best political option that we have. But we should acknowledge that it comes with enormous risks.

One risk is that sacralized national symbols will take on religious undertones. For example, some citizens will find the symbolic power of the flag so potent that they are unwilling to brook expressions of dissent like kneeling during the national anthem. When national symbols are sacralized, political dissent is seen not merely as disrespectful but as sacrilegious.

Another risk is that efforts toward national unity will appropriate and distort religious symbols. Consider the words of a federal judge deciding an Establishment Clause challenge to the symbol of the cross on government property: "The cross has a broadly-understood ancillary meaning as a symbol of military service, sacrifice, and death; it is displayed along with numerous purely secular symbols in an overall context that reinforces its secular message;

and it is historically significant. As a result, the specter of government endorsement of religion or favoring a religion is not apparent, let alone obvious and primary."[26] The attempt to neutralize the power of the Christian symbol of the cross in the service of national unity should concern Christians and non-Christians alike.[27]

A second and related way in which Patel is too optimistic in his appeal for a modest unity is his premise that pluralism includes "a commitment to the common good" (20). We can and must find common ground across our deep differences. But I am far less certain that we can ever share a commitment to "the common good." We disagree about the purposes and ends of our shared political experiment. We disagree about the meaning of life, the nature of a human being, the definition of equality, and the role of happiness. These are not small matters. They prevent us from articulating a nontautological definition of "the common good" for our country and for our neighbors. And they open the door for a political majority to impose its policy preferences under the auspices of "common good" language.

The authors of the First Amendment were attuned to these political realities, even at a time in which those who held political power were far more homogenous than today. We know this in part from the debates over the First Amendment's right of assembly.[28] When the First Congress met to draft amendments to the Constitution, it began by considering language submitted by state delegations. Virginia and North Carolina offered identical amendments: "That the people have a right peaceably to assemble together to consult for the common good, or to instruct their representatives; and that every freeman has a right to petition or apply to the legislature for redress of grievances."[29] The proposals from New York and Rhode Island made one important substitution: they asserted that the people assembled for "their" common good rather than "the" common good.

The distinction between the common good of those assembled and *the* common good did not go unnoticed in the House debates.

When Thomas Hartley of Pennsylvania contended that, with respect to assembly, "every thing that was not incompatible with the
general good ought to be granted," Elbridge Gerry of Massachusetts replied that if Hartley "supposed that the people had a right to
consult for the common good" but "could not consult unless they
met for that purpose," he was in fact "contend[ing] for nothing."[30] The
House voted to adopt the version that referred to "their common
good."[31] The Senate then dropped the "common good" language
completely from the text. But the record of the exchange between
Hartley and Gerry survives, and it suggests that the right of the
people to assemble could not be constrained to a majoritarian
understanding of the common good. This brings me to my second
critique of Patel's argument.

My Pessimism about the Law

My constitutional reflections on Patel's essay are based more on
what is missing from his argument than on what it contains. We get
a hint of that omission from Patel's appeal to former New York City
mayor Michael Bloomberg's defense of Muslims' "constitutional
right to build Cordoba House" (38). Patel endorses Bloomberg's
claims that "the government is bound by the First Amendment of
the Constitution to protect religious expression" and that the government has "a duty of noninterference regarding religious practice"
(39). Even if these claims may accord with an earlier understanding
of the First Amendment, they aren't quite right today.

The key constitutional development that complicates Bloomberg's claims is a 1990 Supreme Court decision, *Employment Division v. Smith*.[32] In that case, two members of the Native American
Church argued that Oregon's refusal to exempt their sacramental
use of peyote from state drug laws violated their free exercise of religion under the First Amendment. The Supreme Court held otherwise: a neutral law of general applicability that applied equally to

religious and nonreligious citizens encountered no resistance from the First Amendment.

The *Smith* decision, which remains good law today, means that Bloomberg's claim that the First Amendment protects religious expression and practice is somewhat imprecise. After *Smith*, the First Amendment's protections for religious liberty are far more circumscribed. New York City could not pass a law banning mosques from a particular area. But it could, under the right circumstances, ban all private structures from the same area. Unless city officials signaled express animosity to Muslims in enacting such an ordinance, they could effectively ban Cordoba House without the slightest concern for religious liberty. And the First Amendment would have nothing to say about it.[33]

Of course, the law is not the only norm that determines the way we treat one another. Appeals to civic aspirations call us to our better selves even when the law allows us to act otherwise. Mayor Bloomberg's speech and Patel's essay both illustrate the genre of writing that appeals to civic aspirations. We need to be reminded that part of our responsibility to each other is to live up to those aspirations. But the law still matters. It is informed by our civic norms, but it also informs those norms. And it currently falls short of the pluralistic ambitions that Patel imagines and that I share.

So what can be done about the law? One place to start is by paying greater attention to the First Amendment's right of assembly. As I mentioned earlier in this response, the authors of the First Amendment believed that the right of assembly extended to countermajoritarian understandings of the common good. In doing so, they hinted at the power of assembly to protect difference and dissent.

The right of assembly also emphasizes the importance of groups. The First Amendment recognizes five individual rights: speech, press, religion, petition, and assembly. Assembly is the only one of these that cannot be exercised by a single individual—it is inherently relational. It reflects the reality that most of us form our identities and beliefs in groups. And its inclusion in the First Amendment means that we cannot fully comprehend our civil liberties without understanding their relational dimension.

Unfortunately, the right of assembly is also one of the First Amendment's least-known provisions: recent surveys conducted by the Newseum Institute found that only one in ten Americans can even name it.[34] Our courts have also forgotten the right of assembly—the Supreme Court has not addressed an assembly claim since the civil rights era.[35] When we think of the civil liberties challenges our nation and its citizens have encountered in recent decades, the absence of the First Amendment's right of assembly is striking.

One reason that our legal and political discourse has neglected the right of assembly is that courts have focused instead on the rights of speech and association, neither of which quite captures the values and norms underlying assembly. Today, free speech doctrine guards the best-known form of assembly—the occasional, temporal gathering that often takes the form of a protest, parade, or demonstration. Meanwhile, the right of association, or, more precisely, what is known as the right of *expressive association*, protects groups across time and place—clubs, churches, and civic organizations.[36]

The free speech framework focuses on the message that a group conveys at the moment of its gathering—the words on a placard, the shouts of a protester, the physical presence of a sit-in. Under what is known as the public forum doctrine, courts today adjudicate government restrictions on protests and demonstrations entirely through the lens of free speech law—the constitutional values and norms of assembly are nowhere to be seen.[37]

The expressive association framework focuses on the group that enables a message. But it focuses only on people who associate in pursuit of some other First Amendment purpose, like speech, press, or religion.[38] This focus instrumentalizes the associational right—it must be enlisted toward some purportedly more significant end. But the ability of citizens to form and maintain their own groups does not depend on some other external purpose. In fact, most of us form significant bonds and beliefs in informal spaces, without agendas or messages.[39]

Consider the example of Muslim Students' Associations.[40] On many college campuses, these groups not only host religious activities but also provide forums for friendships and social interactions. Yet they are unlikely to qualify as "expressive associations" as that doctrine is currently understood because they do not associate for a First Amendment purpose. That leaves them without adequate constitutional protections. This is not merely a hypothetical. In 2008, the New York Police Department sent undercover officers into Muslim Students' Associations on college and university campuses throughout the city. The officers attended the organizations' social events and filed reports about the political and religious conversations they overheard. When investigative reporters broke the story of the NYPD's monitoring program, students who had previously attended MSA meetings stopped coming because they no longer felt safe. These are real First Amendment costs when government action fuels distrust and suspicion among the members of a private group.

Indeed, something is lost when we parse assembly as either speech or association, as our current doctrine does: we miss the inherent connection between a group's existence, its practices, and its message. Treating speech and association separately favors a constitutional analysis that underestimates if not dismisses important First Amendment values like dissent, the fostering of beliefs, the shaping of identity, and informal interactions. These developments leave a gap in our constitutional analysis of claims to group autonomy. And that hole is even more evident now for religious groups, which, as I suggested earlier, find themselves without meaningful religious liberty protections and facing an uphill climb to reclaim those protections.

Here is an example of that gap, from a federal appellate opinion that sets out the current law of the land for a region that covers most of the West Coast: "The requirement that members [of a high school Bible club] possess a true desire to . . . grow in a relationship with Jesus Christ inherently excludes non-Christians" and is therefore a form of invidious discrimination.[41] The right of expressive association does no work at all. The court has no concern for the integrity of the group. And it is not just the Christian group that loses, at least in theory. The reasoning underlying the doctrine of association has broader implications. Let me shift to a different example: gay student groups. These groups were historically of great importance to the gay rights movement in the 1970s.[42] Suppose that the members of one of these groups desired to meet together for social activities—dinners, movies, and other events—at a public university. This group would not qualify as an expressive association. Nor would it qualify under another protection called intimate association—courts have been clear that intimate associations do not extend beyond close family relationships. The gay student group is left without any constitutional protections against majoritarian orthodoxy. That outcome ignores the fact that the very existence of the gay student group, like that of the Christian group, communicates an important message of pluralism and dissent relative to the larger state entity in which it finds itself, something that ought to be of concern to the First Amendment.

In fact, the constitutional distinction that assumes some groups are expressive and some are nonexpressive is difficult to defend. All associative acts have expressive potential: joining, gathering, speaking, and not speaking can all be expressive. The primary reason for protecting groups of people is not expressivism. Groups create spaces for people to form ideas, solidify bonds, and foster values, some of which may be dissenting or countercultural. This function of groups entails risk because it strengthens a genuine pluralism against majoritarian demands for consensus. It resists what the political theorist Nancy Rosenblum has called the liberal state's "logic of congruence," which requires "that the internal life and organization of associations mirror liberal democratic principles and practices."[43]

The need to recover the right of assembly or rehabilitate the right of association is an urgent one. We must insist that the people we entrust to govern us honor basic legal protections, even those that increase the risk of friction, uncertainty, and even instability.

The Challenges and Opportunities for Islam

Patel situates his essay in his experience as a Muslim American, a biographical detail that makes his reflection more than simply an academic exercise. When he asks whether "the self-understanding of America as a Judeo-Christian nation" can shift to include other religious communities, he is asking in part on behalf of his own religious community (43). And when he observes that some of "the groups that are making America increasingly diverse religiously . . . are at each other's throats elsewhere on the planet," he knows that this description also includes his own group (43).

The personal dimensions of the essay strengthen its narrative power. But there are moments when Patel's progressive instincts obscure the stakes. For example, he observes that the September 11, 2001, attacks were "perpetrated by people who called themselves Muslim," but "in reality, the only descriptor that fits is *terrorist*" (44). That doesn't seem quite right to me. Labeling the 9/11 attackers as terrorists does not negate their self-understanding as faithful Muslims. Nor can we ignore the unique challenges in contemporary global politics posed by violence perpetrated in the name of Islam. To be sure, religious adherents of many stripes have committed untold atrocities in the name of faith. But today, militant strands of Islam are slaughtering their neighbors in horrific numbers. It is not enough to insist that these more violent interpreters of a religious tradition simply fall outside it.

On the other hand, Islam, like any other tradition, engages in an ongoing dialogue with itself, what Alasdair MacIntyre has described as an argumentative practice.[44] Practitioners within any tradition-based practice argue with one another about the "best" or "most faithful" interpretation of the antecedent texts, histories, and norms that define the present boundaries of the practice. In a pluralistic society that honors religious freedom and the autonomy of private groups, adherents to these faiths must have the freedom to locate others as outside the acceptable boundaries of the tradition. Patel must be able to say that the perpetrators of the 9/11 attacks are not Muslims, or at least that they are not "true" Muslims. A conservative Christian must be able to say that a progressive Christian is not "orthodox" or "faithful" or properly interpreting sacred texts, and vice versa. Mormons can claim they are Christians, and Southern Baptists can claim that Mormons are not Christians. But in a pluralistic society, the government cannot say where or how these boundaries will be drawn. That restraint on coercion introduces a degree of risk and uncertainty about the nature of any ongoing argumentative practice. We don't always know in advance which side of a contested interpretation will prevail, which means that we don't know which direction a particular tradition will take.

This uncertainty makes the successful integration of Islam into the American experiment an open political question. But we ought not—we cannot—presume the answer to that question. We cannot presume that Islam is incompatible with American democratic practices. We cannot assume that a religious tradition that, like all religious traditions, moves forward as an ongoing dialogue between and among its adherents is without the resources to adapt to this country. We cannot assume that increased numbers of a particular religion lead inevitably to domestic instability and illiberal politics. In an earlier era, anxious Americans made all of these assumptions about Catholics, Jews, Mormons, and dozens of smaller religious sects. And in each case, these faiths eventually found a political compatibility with the American democratic experiment.

The concerns about Islam provide an opportunity for other faiths to demonstrate the ongoing possibility of religious pluralism in this country. For example, as I have argued elsewhere, white Protestants should be taking the lead in advocating for the religious liberty of American Muslims.[45] For much of our country's history, white Protestants established a cultural and legal baseline into which other religious believers had to assimilate. There were some successes, notably the commitment to religious pluralism at the founding of this country at a time when elsewhere in the world people killed and died over inter-Protestant conflicts. But white Protestants also failed to extend religious pluralism to black Protestants, to Mormons, to Catholics, and to other religious sects. The current circumstances provide an opportunity for white Protestants to demonstrate a renewed commitment to religious pluralism, at a time in which they retain a significant amount of cultural privilege even as aspects of that privilege are being weakened.

As Patel notes, some white Protestants, like Franklin Graham and Jerry Falwell Jr., are not exactly rising to the challenge. They sound virulently anti-Muslim in substance and tone. Their posture echoes within the Trump administration and the failed senatorial campaign of Roy Moore in Alabama. But there are signs of hope. The Becket Fund for Religious Liberty makes principled arguments on behalf of a wide range of religious clients, including a Muslim prisoner whose case prevailed at the Supreme Court.[46] Protestant leaders like Russell Moore challenge internal and external constituencies about the need to support religious freedom for American Muslims.[47]

The challenges and opportunities for Islam in this country are ultimately challenges and opportunities for the rest of us, too. They ask whether our historical commitment to religious liberty will withstand powerful forces of fear and bigotry. They ask whether our self-understanding as a leader of the free world will overcome nativist self-interest. And they ask whether the American experiment in pluralism will continue to move forward.

Optimism and Hope

Patel has given us a vision for the political possibility of pluralism in the United States. My commentary has suggested that he is too optimistic about our potential for unity and not concerned enough about the legal protections that we need for our differences. But I am, in the end, mostly in agreement with Patel's optimism.

One reason for my optimism is my belief that we can find common ground even when we don't agree on a common good. We will still need to find a modest unity—the minimal agreement that allows us to live with each other across our disagreements. That modest unity cannot be taken for granted. It must be explained, narrated—and, ultimately, believed. But it is possible to reach that unity, and doing so does not require that we agree on all of the reasons for our agreement. As the philosopher Charles Taylor has argued, "We would agree on the norms while disagreeing on why they were the right norms, and we would be content to live in this consensus."[48]

I remain optimistic about the possibility of finding this consensus in our present circumstances in part because we have found it in our past. One of the great successes of the American experiment has been the ability of its citizens to achieve a modest unity against great odds. We are, to be sure, splintered and polarized in many ways today. But this is not the first time we have encountered profound and unsettling disagreement. Consider, for example, the aspirational language of the Declaration of Independence. As I have written elsewhere, "America's founders, of course, did not actually agree that all men (to say nothing of women) were created equal. The boundaries of 'liberty' were contested, and 'happiness' evoked a civic-mindedness that not everyone shared."[49] Nor did our differences stop there: "Lest we think that only words divided us in past times, we might remember that Puritans executed Quakers in the Massachusetts Bay Colony in the 17th century, race riots and labor unrest led to hundreds of deaths in the 19th and 20th centuries, and 620,000 Americans died at the hands of other Americans during the Civil War."[50]

Despite our past failures to resolve all of our differences peacefully, we have usually managed to find our way toward a modest unity. The Declaration of Independence closes with words less known than those at the beginning: "And for the support of this Declaration, with a firm reliance on the protection of divine Providence, we mutually pledge to each other our Lives, our Fortunes and our sacred Honor." Today, an increasing number of Americans reject the premise of "divine Providence." We may well argue about the meaning and salience of the words in our founding documents. So did the founders of our country, and so have most Americans who have followed after them. But perhaps some of my optimism comes from believing that the notion of "mutually pledg[ing] to each other our Lives" remains possible.

I am optimistic because I have friends like Eboo Patel. His deeply held beliefs and practices differ from my own as a Christian.[51] But our mutual commitment to civic friendship makes our coexistence not only possible but also joyful. Our broader societal differences are not without their costs—they make communication more difficult, politics more strained, and stability more volatile. Nor are all of our differences likely to be overcome—even as we work to bridge relational difference, we will not always surmount ideological difference. But bridging relational difference is no small matter, and it can lead to authentic friendships across ideological difference. It reminds us that people are usually more complex than the labels we attach to them, and that sometimes the things we hold in common are deeper than we realize.

10

Plural America Needs Myths
An Essay in Foundational Narratives in Response to Eboo Patel

Laurie L. Patton

The Issue: The Future of Minority Religious Communities in America

In his *Out of Many Faiths*, Eboo Patel argues that there is an urgency to questions about the role of minority religious communities in America, of which Islam is a primary example. His questions are about the relationship between the particularity of those communities and the common life that we share as Americans. Will those communities be able to withstand and conquer prejudice? Will their contributions to the community be recognized? When America describes itself religiously, might it continue the shift it has been making—from a primarily Christian nation, to a Judeo-Christian nation, to a nation that includes many more religious groups than Christians and Jews? Most importantly for this mythologist and historian of religion interested in interfaith relations, "if such a shift occurs, how will we know it is happening, and what things (symbols, policies, narratives, and so on) will actually change?" (43).

I argue in this response to Patel's work that we will know when that shift has occurred when we have foundational stories—we might even call them "myths"—that are part of our common cultural practice. In taking up the "narrative and symbol" side of Patel's question, I am leaving it to other respondents to engage the policy side of the issues. In addition to the crucial place of policy, I think, as Patel does, that it is important to consider the hard *cultural* work that is necessary in order to move beyond "diversity" to "pluralism." If we pay attention to the artists and storytellers whom Patel mentions in chapter 5, then we will see the kinds of cultural boundary crossings that become allowable and welcome stories and other cultural artifacts that become "tellable" over time. These will include what we might call an "expressible pluralism." As Diana Eck writes, diversity is simply a demographic fact, whereas pluralism is a hard-won achievement, in which difference is engaged toward positive ends.[1] How do those ends become established and known? I argue here that they become known partly through narrative and partly through everyday ethics expressed by those narratives.

Pluralism Needs Myths

Let me turn first to the question of narrative. As a mythologist, I analyze myth in terms of what Gananath Obeyesekere calls "a social argument."[2] For Obeyesekere, myths are powerful narratives with multiple points of view that speak to broader, complex social fabrics. The narratives that last and become truly foundational or "classic" are ones that are the most complex, and therefore the most interpretable on multiple levels. Another way of putting this is that myths that become foundational are deeply hospitable, in the sense that the literary critic Tzvetan Todorov taught us;[3] they constantly invite interpretations. If the social project of moving from "religious diversity" to "religious pluralism" is to survive and thrive, it needs not only policies but also forms of social argumentation—that is, myths or foundational narratives. In other words, pluralism needs myths.

This perspective on myth builds on many eminent mythologists' perspectives on myths. They argue that myths need pluralism

in order to survive. As Wendy Doniger puts it in her first method-
ological work about interpreting mythology,

> The pluralism of India may also provide a model for the plural-
> ism of the scholar of religion. If one can ask many different good
> questions about any single myth, and one can answer any of
> these questions in a variety of good ways, it makes sense to
> try several different approaches—structuralism, Freudianism,
> Marxism—to round up the usual hermeneutical suspects. The
> metaphor of the microscope illustrates the uses of the multidimen-
> sional approach: you must constantly change the scale in which
> you view any particular phenomenon, for there are always at
> least two levels above and two levels below what you are looking
> at at any given moment.[4]

Later, Doniger argues for telescopes as well as microscopes as
important tools that help us see the larger picture and context of a
myth. Microscopes show the different scales on which myths can
and should be interpreted, whereas telescopes allow us to see the
historical, social, ideological, and other factors that have influenced
its telling. The context of any foundational narrative is inevitably
plural.

In looking at this dynamic between pluralism and myths, we
might take an obvious example from Patel's work: the myth of
the Four Chaplains. As Patel writes, this narrative is "a naturally
dramatic and inspiring story in which two Protestant pastors, a
Catholic priest, and a Jewish rabbi gave up their life jackets to
scared soldiers on the sinking USS *Dorchester*, a U.S. naval vessel
that had been hit by a torpedo from a German U-boat. After saving
the lives of these soldiers, the chaplains then joined arms and
jumped to their deaths in the roiling ocean, each with the prayers of
his own religion on his lips" (71). This myth, inadequate though it
is by today's cultural standards, helped America see itself as a more
plural nation.

Patel reminds us that, historically, many groups and organizations have focused on the cultural work of pluralizing America

and thereby making a more expansive religious definition of the nation. In the case of the Four Chaplains, the relevant group is the National Conference of Christians and Jews, whose members worked hard during World War II and beyond to push back against the definition of America as an exclusively Christian nation, an ideal that even liberals like Franklin Delano Roosevelt embraced. Instead, they concentrated on calling it a Judeo-Christian nation and took advantage of the compelling story of the Four Chaplains. As Patel puts it, "Policy makers and interfaith activists quickly recognized the symbolic potency of this event" (71). And a variety of cultural products followed that contributed to the myth: articles, tributes, essays, postage stamps, sermons, and Warner Brothers films, as well as a chapel to the Four Chaplains—their name capitalized to honor their heroic status (71).

Through the deft use of these stories, the term *Judeo-Christian* was instituted, and an alliance between Christians and Jews became paramount in the United States. This nomenclature helped to change, albeit partially and imperfectly, one of the bloodiest and most violent interreligious relationships in human history. There are many social critiques one could make about the term *Judeo-Christian* in 2017: It does not include anyone beyond those two traditions, even Islam, which is another member of an Abrahamic faith. It is a term that only Christians would use, as it refers to the Jewish roots of Christianity. Jews find themselves erased in their particularity in the use of such a term, because their tradition is only represented as "background" or "origin" for the emergence of Christianity. However imperfect it is for 2017, it remains a popular term, and for the latter half of the twentieth century it provided a much-needed corrective to a singularly Christian narrative that had been regnant up to that point. Such a movement needed the myth of the Four Chaplains to help cement that symbolism. This story is one powerful example, then, of the way that pluralism needs myths. The myth of the Four Chaplains is a form of social argumentation about pluralism itself. This and similar stories are made up of extraordinary acts of individuals, grounded in history but capable of being interpreted symbolically in a number of complex ways.

Pragmatic Pluralism as Everyday Ethics

Do we need only extraordinary acts to begin working on this question? How do we begin to tell a myth? Can the ideal of pluralism that is contained in American civil religion really be strong enough to carry its own mythology? Can it engage in the project referring to and revising the various foundational narratives that are compelling ways of thinking about pluralism? I think that it can and it should. However, the narratives need to be formed from local stories about everyday acts, as well as grand stories about heroic acts such as those of the Four Chaplains. Most mythological traditions emerge out of artistic and storytelling activities of the culture itself. The less self-conscious the mythology is, the better. In other words, myths need to be about everyday ethics of pluralistic behavior.

When speaking and writing about this interdependency in public intellectual situations, I refer frequently to Rabbi Jonathan Sacks's idea of the "dignity of difference."[5] In his view, a focus on commonality is not enough. We still *need* difference in many human relationships—such as trade and barter between relative equals. In the example of trade, we feel the powerful effect of difference immediately: if you have what I have, then the activity of barter makes no sense and will not succeed. For example, if we both have apples, I will try to buy out your store of apples or beat you as the competition in selling to others who want to buy apples. If I have apples and you have oranges, then we can trade and our relationship will continue. The activity of barter needs difference in order to thrive. I must have something different from what you have in order to trade at all.

Biodiversity works on the same principle. The most biodiverse climates, such as the Galapagos Islands or the Piedmont in the southern United States, are biodiverse because different species have formed interdependent relationships. No single species has become dominant, what we now call an "invasive species." Invasive species create biological likeness on a mass scale, and the differences that created the ecosystem cease to become productive or needed.

The same can also work with religious difference. This concept pushes us to see that we might not just tolerate difference but in fact need it. It pushes us to see that in the United States we exist within the context of a civil religion that asks us to be dependent on our religious differences, and it declares that interdependence as a positive fact. The phrase I have been using to develop Sacks's idea further is "pragmatic pluralism." Elsewhere I have defined this as when "one religion needs another tradition to be itself."[6] In their relationships in the public square, where, as Patel puts it, people orient around the sacred differently,[7] religious traditions nonetheless still need each other to be who they are in their differences.

Most importantly, we need foundational narratives—myths— to describe these situations, honor this fact, and invite interpretation. There have been many moments in the work I have done with interreligious actors in Atlanta, in Durham, and in several different cities in India that have revealed powerful narratives, even transformative narratives, of this kind of relationship. While they have come up in a variety of contexts, both large and small, these narratives never fail to move the group assembled in ways that are markedly different from your run-of-the-mill story of interreligious collaboration. In that sense, they have the power to be foundational narratives, or mythologies of pluralism.

I have begun to collect stories of this kind of transformative interdependence in order to demonstrate what I mean. They are, in my view, the building blocks of mythic traditions for interreligious collaboration. They are not necessarily master narratives, in the sense that Jean-Francois Lyotard[8] used the term, but they are, as I mentioned earlier, "hospitable narratives"[9]—ones that allow interreligious actors to imagine differently and to continue to act. They tend to be about everyday, ethical acts that show and nurture that interdependence.

What Makes an Effective Myth?

Before we turn to examples of effective, transformational narratives, let us delve deeper into what might make a good myth and why. I see four key criteria. Effective interfaith narratives

- invoke a wider sense of a "we";
- have compelling poetic imagery;
- depict ethical actions to be reflected on and interpreted in a multitude of ways;
- portray compelling moments of identity formation.

Let me begin with the first—the wider sense of a "we." Eck, also cited by Patel, writes about this wider sense of a "we" when she writes of her own transformation in *A New Religious America*. What began with Christian churches among the maples in New England has expanded to "the sacred mountains and the homelands of the Native peoples, the Peace Pagoda amid maples in Massachusetts, the mosque in the cornfields outside Toledo, the Hindu temples pitched atop the hills of Pittsburgh and Chicago, the old and new Buddhist temples of Minneapolis."[10] She has reimagined the landscape of America and started to call all of it "home." That wider sense of "we" cannot simply be added on but rather must be fully understood as part of a new cultural imaginary. This is what Lord Herbert of Cherbury started to accomplish even in the sixteenth century, when he argued that the human "we" should include non-Christians. (And he paid dearly for it.) As Patel reminds us, the stories should not be all positive, whitewashing the struggle of what it took to build each moment of religious inclusion. Such narratives should also chronicle what it took each community to become part of the landscape.

The second—that narrative should have a compelling poetics—
would seem to be straightforward enough. Many scholars have argued that myths possess a kind of poetic force—a series of images
and juxtapositions that intrigue our imaginations and startle us
into asking what it means to invite further thought. The Four
Chaplains is that story because we want to know what they were
thinking, how they came to be united in that space for that instant,
how they came to the decision that they did. We tell the story not
only because it is about an ultimate self-sacrifice, although we
should of course begin there. We also tell it because it is human,
filled with the personalities and flaws and quibbles of each of the
actors.

This poetics, I believe, is what Justice Felix Frankfurter means
by "cohesive sentiment" (24)—a recognition of the human rather
than a simple sentimentality. In this sense, the imagery itself, of four
men reciting prayers as they sink into the ocean, has a human poetics, as does their decision to distribute their own life jackets on that
day. The story is a simple but deep recognition of the human. The
details of their lives have this poetics too, such as the hill in Deer-
ing, New Hampshire, being renamed Clark Summit because it was
a place where one of the reverends, Clark V. Poling, used to go to
make important life decisions. However, the poetics of such a story
need not be as dramatic as four chaplains saving lives on a sinking
ship. They can also be more everyday—the larger point is that they
must intrigue our imagination and offer us possibilities for reflection
and reinterpretation.

The third criterion—exemplary action—is related to this compelling poetics. The actions in the myth must stand out or be what
cognitive scientists call "counterintuitive." As Pascal Boyer, Robert
McCauley, Thomas Lawson, and other cognitive scientists remind
us,[11] an effective religious symbol is usually something quite ordinary but that also possesses one exceptional trait or characteristic
that helps us remember it. The actions of the Four Chaplains were
unremarkable as those of people organizing large groups of men

and handing out provisions and supplies. However, the context of their actions was the one element that made them extraordinary. One survivor of the torpedoed ship recounts the straightforward act of handing over life jackets as such: "It was the finest thing I have seen or hope to see this side of heaven," said John Ladd, who saw the chaplains' selfless act. "Never was there a more sublime moment than that moment."[12]

It is important to be clear here. Although the example I have been using, the story of the Four Chaplains, is morally exemplary, not all stories of interfaith engagement need be so. Rather, they need to focus on spiritual interdependence and its possibilities for human flourishing—ways in which such flourishing can be inhibited as well as encouraged. They can also be everyday, mundane examples, as are some of the stories I will tell later—stories of cooking, teaching, singing, and so on.

Finally, effective interfaith stories involve moments of identity formation—when one actor or actors in the story understand themselves differently. Frequently such narratives involve moments of arrival after a long journey. Bruce Lincoln writes compellingly of this particularly (although by no means exclusively) American way of telling a story, noting that transformation often occurs after such a journey has been completed. In his essay "Mythic Narrative and Cultural Diversity in American Society,"[13] Lincoln focuses on the movie *Avalon*, in which the Krichinsky family narrates the arrival of their ancestor Sam Krichinsky on American soil. Lincoln goes on to offer a more general outline of American mythology that involves a transformative (in both positive and negative senses) voyage, a discovery of the land, and, finally, an encounter with the previous inhabitants of the land, who may have a better claim to it. Patel tells many such stories in his own work, such as the journey of American Muslim slaves or the difficult, life-changing journeys of those Muslims whose lives were interrupted by the recent travel ban involving seven predominantly Muslim countries. After their journeys, they know the world differently, and they know something about themselves that they would not have known without that journey. This new knowledge about the self and world can be political, social, economic, spiritual, or psychological.

As so many mythologists have taught us, the role of context in the telling of these narratives is essential. The narratives discussed later were all either told by the actors themselves in informal contexts, such as the art historian at the Breman Museum, or picked up by the press at moments of great public difficulty, such as in the aftermath of 9/11. Like most myths, such narratives would be effective in both formal and informal contexts of telling, and they should engage both registers along a continuum. Some may be local myths that are told in city and town councils, in classrooms, or in religious services, while others might be shared by written publications or a televised, streamed, or virtual event. In each context of telling, the medium would have as much to do with the efficacy of the narrative as the context.

It might also be helpful here to think about what might be an ineffective narrative. First, we can argue that the mere statement of facts and figures will not change the American narrative to make it more inclusive. The mere fact that Turkish Muslims helped rebuild Dayton, Ohio, will not stir the American imagination into telling a different story, nor will the fact that fifteen thousand doctors who are now healing people in rural and urban America hail from the seven countries named in the travel ban. However, what will make a difference is the combination of these facts with effective stories about these facts: widespread circulation of compelling narratives about them, their struggles, and their triumphs. Compelling narratives are facts and figures that are retold in such a way so that, as Patel writes, they make connections with previous narratives (26) and become part of a familiar landscape of community.

Second, myths that involve the kind of mental shortcuts that Patel writes about will not help in expanding American identity. They may be very effective in the short run in consolidating particular identities, but they will not take root in the long run in a genuinely plural society. Patel, citing the work of Daniel Kahneman and Amos Tversky, makes use of the idea of "mental maps" of the world, which involve several elements: the use of stereotypes; the development of judgments based only on the information available; the priming of the brain to think of further examples only like the initial ones that are given; the use of confirmation bias, or the active search for information that confirms current mental maps; and the automatic search for causality, in which an easy explanation is offered for particular phenomena, even when none exists. Patel gives many examples of this kind of mental shortcut being used in political rhetoric. He argues that the stronger narratives are ones where the opposite occurs: they explode stereotypes; they invite reflection, not judgment; they engage the reader in both confirming and disconfirming examples; they do not give an automatic cause-and-effect answer.

It is also important to be clear about the role of myths and their capacity for revision. Because powerful stories invite reflection and reinterpretation, and each of them is human and incomplete, yet compelling in the ways I outlined earlier, there may be retellings of myths that are more adequate to the times. The story of the Four Chaplains could be read as too focused on the Jewish and Christian story and in need of an update to include indigenous people, Muslims, Sikhs, Hindus, and many other religious minorities. A myth is not a perfect narrative; rather, it is a reinterpretable one.

In sum: effective interfaith myths invite reflection. They do not dissolve social tensions but instead ask us to explore them. In doing so, they encourage us to think about a wider sense of "we." They do so with language and imagery that is poetically compelling. They also do so by depicting actions to be reflected on, and they clearly show crucial moments in identity formation. They avoid sentimentality, eschew the mental shortcuts of preconditioned attitudes, and connect with earlier effective narratives. What would such stories actually look like? The next section will explore some possibilities.

Pluralism's Compelling Interests: Telling the Stories

So far, I have argued two basic points: (1) pluralism needs a mythology, and (2) that mythology can be made up of stories of everyday ethics that acknowledge and engage interdependence. I want to turn now to Patel's outline of the compelling interests that a framework of pluralism helps us to advance, and use it as a framework for suggesting several examples of foundational narratives—ones that could become myths of everyday interfaith ethics. Here are these interests as Patel sees them (15):

- Guard against religious preference and establishment and continue the American ideal of free exercise for all faith communities.
- Develop a national narrative that is inclusive of our new social reality of high levels of religious diversity.
- Reduce prejudice and openly welcome the myriad contributions of multiple communities (civic, professional, cultural, and so on).
- Facilitate positive relations between diverse religious communities, guarding against conflict and strengthening social cohesion.
- Encourage particular religious communities to harmonize their distinctive traditions with national ideals such as civic participation and pluralism.

Patel sees two different reasons for these interests being compelling. The first is a civic one: a democracy requires the contributions of its citizens, and prejudice and discrimination not only violate the identities of directly affected groups but also hurt the broader society by impeding their contributions on a variety of fronts (14). The second interest is more directly related to the narrative interests of this essay. Patel refers to Philip Gorski's *American Covenant* to describe it:

"To be part of a tradition," [Gorski] states, "is to know certain stories, read certain books, admire certain people, and care about certain things. It is to knowingly enter into an ongoing conversation, a conversation that precedes one's birth and continues on after one's death" [*American Covenant*, 4].

The civil religious tradition was first invoked with reference to the United States by the sociologist Robert Bellah in 1967. Bellah spoke of it as the "religious dimension" of the "political realm" and the "founding myth" of our national community. It stands separate from people's traditional faiths but draws freely from religious language to sacralize national symbols. (23)

Unlike religious nationalism or radical secularism, such civil religious traditions do not manipulate religious symbols in the service of the nation, as religious nationalism does. Nor do they muzzle the inspirations of religious Americans, as radical secularism does (xiv).

As mentioned earlier, I have been collecting stories that focus on religious interdependence, that pragmatic pluralism in which "one religion needs another religion to be itself." Many of them have the narrative properties that I described earlier and illustrate the kinds of principles that Patel has outlined above. In what follows, I will be choosing stories that I believe, and many of my students have found, are compelling narratives that helps us move forward in making interreligious change.

I should be clear about my own stake in these stories. All of them involve Jewish communities in some way or another. When I chose them as paradigmatically American stories appropriate for this commentary, I was surprised to see that this Jewish theme emerged. But then I became less surprised. Although I am a scholar of Indian religions and an interfaith leader, Judaism is my tradition of choice. As a Jew, I am naturally most compelled by the ways in which the Jewish tradition allows for that "dignity of difference" that Jonathan Sacks writes about. Keeping Jewish identity while at the same time engaging with other traditions has been a theme of Midrashim, or exegetical narratives, and Jewish ritual commentaries for centuries. However, while these stories are compelling to me for the Jewish elements, they are also compelling for the larger reasons of plural engagement so prominent in this book. I could replace the chosen powerful American narratives involving Jews and members of other religious traditions with just as many narratives involving Muslims and Christians, Hindus and Christians, Hindus and Muslims, Sikhs and Native Americans, and so on. This essay is an invitation to others to do so.

I should mention here that, while I have chosen stories about Jews interacting with other religious traditions, there is a powerful set of stories emerging about the power of the "nones"—those with no religious affiliation. For example, atheist or humanist societies are increasingly involved in and visible at disaster relief efforts. In addition, as political scientist Ashutosh Varshney has taught us, the secular, civic sphere in interreligious engagements provides a crucial base from which different religious traditions can interact with each other, as well as with secularists or "nones."[14] The next step in interreligious storytelling might include these groups in a more explicit way. It might also acknowledge the crucial role that civic spaces play in pragmatic pluralism.

THE FIRST NARRATIVE: REEMBRACING THE PRIESTHOOD AFTER A CLASS AT A JEWISH MUSEUM

The first of Patel's compelling interests is to "guard against religious preference and establishment and continue the American ideal of free exercise for all faith communities."

How do everyday actions help us protect the right to free exercise? One story from Atlanta outlines particularly intriguing possibilities. A Jewish museum in Atlanta, the Breman Museum, regularly sponsors adult education classes. In the mid-2000s, the classes ranged from specifically Jewish topics, such as Passover Observance or the History of the Jews in Europe, to more general ones, such as Introduction to the Art of Western Civilization, which involved a natural but not exclusive acknowledgment of Jewish contributions to that history. One woman from a large Atlanta synagogue, Jessica Sandler (not her real name), was going through a midlife transition, and she decided that one of the things she could do was use her art historical background to teach the Introduction to the Art of Western Civilization class. She dusted off the syllabus for an earlier class that she had taught, and began the lectures. Because it was a general class, she included more Jewish content than a Christian or secular professor might but didn't make it a course exclusively about Jewish art history.

The course went well. The students came from a wide variety of walks of life. Some students were more voluble than others were. Although it was an evening course, there was a lot of focused energy in the room. Some would sit up in the front and try to answer every question Jessica asked. Some would come in clearly tired after a long day's work and sit in the back, quietly listening. The class progressed through the medieval period, the Renaissance, the Reformation, the Enlightenment, the Romantic response, and the advent of modern art and the avant-garde movements.

At the end of the class, one of the students who had been at the back of the room for the whole class, a modestly dressed, middle-aged man, came up to Jessica to thank her for the class. "I am so grateful for the class," he said. "You've restored my faith in my own vocational calling." Jessica was surprised. He had not really said much during the class, and she didn't have a keen sense of him as a student. "How did that happen?" she said. "Well," he replied, "I am a priest. I had lost my sense of why I was a priest, and what the Catholic Church really meant to me after all. But your course taught me the history of Western art, and particularly sacred art, from a Jewish perspective. And once I read the history of Christian art with Jewish eyes, I began to love my tradition again. I think I needed to see things as a Jew in order to get to know my tradition afresh, and become a better priest."

This is an inspiring, everyday story. It is about a person who, by seeing a different perspective on his own choice of vocation, was able to reclaim it. Even more importantly, it is about a Catholic understanding a Jewish perspective. Jewish views of Christianity range from outreach and ecumenicism to downright distrust, based on a long history of violence as well as the supercessionist theology of Christianity that teaches that the inferior Jewish law must be replaced by the superior Christian love. For the priest, returning to a place where none of these factors were at play actually freed him to reembrace what mattered in his own faith. The fact that Jessica did not even know that this change was occurring in the mind and heart of her student made it even more compelling. It was a fulfillment of Maimonides's ideal of charity, where one does not even know the recipient of one's good deed.

But why would such a story help guard against religious establishment? I think it can do so for an important reason. It's a story about the fact that the honoring of a single tradition in the public square (in this case, the smaller public of the classroom) is less powerful than the interdependence of two (or more) traditions. To put it another way, American civic space allowed the teaching of a class about the history of art in Western civilization from within the confines of a well-established Jewish museum in a state that is predominantly Protestant evangelical in a country founded by Puritans. That was the winning combination for the priest as well as the teacher. More importantly for our purposes, it underscored the interdependence of religious traditions, as well as the fact that people can participate in a variety of public spheres—many of them not even their own—and become transformed by them. They can even become refreshed in their own tradition's beliefs and practices by their engagement of difference.

THE SECOND NARRATIVE: RECIPROCITY
NEED NOT INCLUDE AFFECTION

Patel writes that a third compelling interest is to "develop a national narrative that is inclusive of our new social reality of high levels of religious diversity."

Patel rightly suggests that Eck's understanding of a "we" needs to be incorporated into our narratives. But that is a very hard thing to do, given the increasing focus on multicultural identities, as people in communities that understand themselves as vulnerable can easily be averse to such narratives of inclusion. Why include others when we are worried about our own rights being trampled and, in many cases, keeping our community safe? (The extreme of this concern for one's own fragile minority community is what some call "the Olympics of Oppression.") Relatedly, there is a fear of admitting the pluralism within one's own community, for it would undermine the idea that, in an American democracy, a community is coherent enough to claim an identity, and that identity and the members of that community should be respected. For this reason, narratives that reflect our new social reality of high levels of diversity are particularly challenging. Stories involving not only difference but also the maintenance of that difference are difficult to find and to tell—on the local and the national scales.

But there are indeed inspiring examples of such pluralism. I encountered one such narrative when at an interfaith conference in Spartanburg-Greenville, South Carolina, an area that has a long-term Muslim and Jewish population. The purpose of the conference was in part to tell the history of those and other minority communities. Yes, they had a history, and many were surprised at how long that history was. As the conference wound up, both Jewish and Muslim representatives approached me and said, "We're too small to have only a kosher outfit, or only a halal outfit. So we collaborate instead on both kosher and halal. It's a tradition in South Carolina, and we love telling that story!"

That small state narrative breaks many stereotypes. The first is that of South Carolina itself as a place of backward, narrow-minded people. Instead, the pride of the state, and of the city, was interfaith collaboration, and the story was frequently told. The second is that Jews and Muslims don't get along, no matter where they are. This narrative begins to provide an answer to one of the questions Patel poses near the beginning of his book: "In what ways will minority religious communities themselves change as they plant themselves in American soil? Will the groups that are making America increasingly diverse religiously, some of which are at each other's throats elsewhere on the planet, relate positively to one another here in the United States, or will they carry conflicts from elsewhere with them?" (43). One response to this question is that America, at its best, can provide a place in which those communities are able to change and begin to relate positively to each other. But this story depicts something more than simply positive relations; it shows pragmatic pluralism at its best—the Jewish community and the Muslim community need each other to be themselves in order to create the most affordable food preparation in their city according to religious laws. Do Muslims and Jews in South Carolina agree on what should be done in Israel-Palestine? Probably not. But they can and do create long-term partnerships on eating.

These kinds of stories about pragmatic pluralism emerge within traditions as well as between them. One story was told to me by my stepfather-in-law, now deceased. As he narrated it, "In one small town in upstate New York, relationships between Orthodox and Reform Jews were very bad. One winter day the Orthodox synagogue burned down. About a week after the fire, the rabbi of the Orthodox synagogue was surprised to see the Reform rabbi at his door, with a large donation. 'Without you being Orthodox, we couldn't be Reform,' he said. 'So you had better rebuild.'"

This brief exchange is not a narrative of reconciliation and dialogue—far from it. It doesn't tell the story of how the Orthodox and Reform rabbis are now going to get along in the wake of tragedy. Far from it; the story is instead an acknowledgment of ongoing difference. It is also an acknowledgment that the Orthodox and Reform communities needed each other to maintain that difference and to continue to be themselves. For my father-in-law, this story was a form of humor, a way of making gentle fun of the schisms within his own Jewish faith. He mentioned in passing that the story is told frequently, and there are now variations on it. I thought to myself then that myths naturally tend to generate variations if their forms of social argument are compelling enough. For me, the story was a moving illustration of a way in which what starts as a humorous narrative can actually become a narrative of inclusion. And in this case, it is reflective of our religious diversity even within a tradition—one of the most difficult forms of diversity to embrace and maintain.

Neither of these stories is a "national" story in the sense that Patel writes about. However, they are ones that feature the civic entities and larger purposes of both states (South Carolina pride) and towns (the interfaith traditions of Spartanburg-Greenville, or the need for both Orthodox and Reform synagogues in an upstate New York town). And they can serve as models for the kinds of national narratives that might spontaneously develop, in which an American town or city is also a religiously diverse town or city, and stories we tell reflect that new reality.

THE THIRD NARRATIVE: COOKING IN RESPONSE TO JENIN
Patel reminds us that the fourth compelling interest is to "reduce prejudice and openly welcome the myriad contributions of multiple communities (civic, professional, cultural, and so on)," thereby increasing social capital. Social capital has been notoriously difficult to define, and there is no real scholarly agreement on a precise definition. We might turn to the Organization for Economic Cooperation and Development for a general definition: "networks together with shared norms, values and understandings that facilitate cooperation within or among groups."[15] These networks are also beneficial to both the individuals and society.

One moving story about social capital concerns an interfaith women's group called Interfaith Sisters in Atlanta, Georgia. (A subsequent group, Women's Interfaith Network, was founded in 2013.) The story centers on an event that occurred in 2002, just after what is now known as the Battle of Jenin. The Israeli army had gone into the Palestinian camp of Jenin as part of Operation Defensive Shield. Israeli authorities had reported that the camp was a place from which numerous attacks against Israeli villages and civilians were being launched. When the army entered the camp with infantry, commando forces, and helicopters, it was met with fierce resistance by Palestinian militants who had built a series of booby traps. Israel responded by clearing the booby traps with armored bulldozers. What then occurred was a media storm. Reports of atrocities, mass killings, and mass graves spread throughout the international news outlets. Most of these reports did not turn out to be accurate. The final count, confirmed by both Palestinian and Israeli officials, was that between fifty-two and fifty-four Palestinians and twenty-three Israeli forces died in the battle. However, the damage was done, and Palestinians continued to protest what they felt was brutal treatment at the hands of the Israeli army.

Back in Atlanta, Interfaith Sisters had always felt that their strength was that they were Muslim, Jewish, and Christian, as well as Hindu and Buddhist. They met on a regular basis, read books together, and exchanged stories of their faith and rituals. Even though they had a larger, more expansive interfaith perspective, the group also admired the Jewish-Muslim organization in Israel-Palestine called the Parents Circle Family Forum, which was formed by grieving families who have lost children in the ongoing conflict and who gather together to share the stories of their loss.

While members of Interfaith Sisters did not necessarily lose loved ones as a result of the Battle of Jenin, they still felt it their obligation to come together and to grieve the losses in that region in response to the violence. But when they gathered to talk, they found that they could not agree. The Jewish women felt that they had to defend Israel against false reports, and the Palestinian women felt that they had to show solidarity with those Palestinians subjected to violence, no matter what the situation on the ground. Despite several attempts, they could not discuss the issue without creating profound alienation between them.

This situation was new for this strong, long-standing, interfaith group, who had gathered a great deal of respect in Atlanta, already a city with a strong interfaith focus and engagement. They weren't sure what to do next. But their solution was not to disband. Nor was it even to take a break. Rather, it was to continue to meet, but not to talk about Jenin or even Israel-Palestine. Instead, they decided to cook each other food. They stayed together by cooking together. They found a way to continue the relationship, as well as to maintain social capital—those networks that were so beneficial to them and to larger Atlanta. They became the "cooking interfaith sisters of Atlanta," and they began to see food preparation and sharing as a way of maintaining relationships when the only other possible options were silence or disbandment. As one member of the group put it, "Now it is at least cooking silence, and not hostile silence."[16]

In the terms of Patel's compelling interest, these women made a conscious decision right at the moment when they would have otherwise been tempted to revert to "mental shortcuts" that confirmed the stereotypes of Israelis and Palestinians, Jews and Muslims. They decided to do the opposite and acknowledge the contributions of each other's culture through meal preparation. That is, for Patel, the essence of building social capital, and their choice creates a powerful narrative that could be told as a foundational one.

THE FOURTH NARRATIVE: FINDING A PLACE
TO PRAY BEFORE DANCE CLASS

Patel finishes his list of compelling interests with the idea that we might "facilitate positive relations between diverse religious communities, guarding against conflict and strengthening social cohesion."

It is always a good thing to foster positive relations. But what are the kinds of positive relations that last? Dialogue, cooperative ecumenical festivities, and Thanksgiving rituals are all important moments in any interfaith community. However, they must be based on something more than an episodic engagement. There are several narratives that focus instead on the sharing of space that could provide us with models. The most dramatic ones emerge after disaster, such as the story of the Four Chaplains, mentioned earlier, or the recent gesture in late January 2017 of a group of Jews in Victoria, Texas, who gave Muslims the keys to their synagogue after their mosque was burned down.

The Victoria example highlights what Varshney also emphasizes: that ongoing social relations between civic leaders actually lead to a reduction in intercommunal violence when communities are threatened by disruptive events.[17] In his study of communal peace and violence in several cities in India, Varshney looked at what community structures were present in cities where rioting broke out after a violent episode in a long-standing Hindu-Muslim controversy, and he compared them to the structures that were present in the cities where rioting did not break out in order to determine what accounted for the difference. He discovered that the cities that avoided riots have civic leaders who call each other, report on actual events, and quash rumors that could lead to group violence.

And this is exactly what happened in Victoria. Dr. Shahid Hashmi was delighted but not surprised when his friend and colleague Dr. Gary Branfman came to his house and gave him the keys to temple B'Nai Israel in Victoria, where he was a member. They knew each other as fellow surgeons, and they could immediately act in unison to bring the two communities together to address the issue. This friendship had the added effect of bringing the Muslim community and the larger community together. Commenting on the fact that there were several churches in the town but only one mosque and one synagogue, the rabbi said, "As Jews we have to feel for the Muslim community."[18]

Yet in my mind, the less dramatic examples might be even more lasting and run even deeper in fostering these positive relations. The story of the synagogue in Riverdale, New York, where a Muslim girl was allowed to pray after school is also a powerful example.[19] Dinar Puspita was an Indonesian exchange student in an increasingly Orthodox neighborhood, and her high school was fifteen blocks from the Riverdale Muslim center. She would not be able to get there and get back to class for her theater and dance rehearsals. Nor was she able to pray at the school itself. So her host, Naomi Erickson, asked if the local Jewish center could give her a space. And the rabbi was happy to comply, showing her a few empty rooms in the center where she might be able to perform her afternoon prayers.

Dinar decided to pray in a long hallway with memorial plaques honoring the families of members and donors. The *New York Times* story on this issue emphasized the ordinariness of this event, noting Rabbi Rosenblatt's comment, "I never understood what the big deal was," he said. "Somebody's child from halfway around the world needs a place to worship." The article ends, "Still, Rabbi Rosenblatt addressed the issue at a service, telling his congregation that he was not only comfortable but proud that someone felt a holiness in this place. 'It's the first time I remember applause after a sermon,' he said."[20]

The Riverdale story involved a plain-spoken response to a plain, ordinary need. However, the work of positive engagement is also quite ordinary. There are, of course, many occasions when congregations share space in America. Examples abound in which Jewish congregations are loaned space in a Christian church. There are even examples of such churches making sure the Ner Tamid, or the eternal flame so essential to a synagogue's identity, is kept lit in the part of the church where the Jewish congregation meets. But we have rarely told these stories of such ongoing interfaith cooperation. We have rarely recorded the conversations between the congregants when such space is shared, or the positive relationships between religious leaders or congregants that result.

THE FIFTH NARRATIVE: SINGING THE PSALMS
AFTER SEPTEMBER 11

The second compelling interest is to "encourage particular religious communities to harmonize their distinctive traditions with national ideals such as civic participation and pluralism."

The encouragement to harmonize can emerge in extreme as well as not so extreme situations. The American tragedy of 9/11 gives us an important story to reflect on.[21] One day not long after 9/11, the recovery of the victims' remains had reached a particular stage. It was time to store whatever remains there were in a refrigerator truck before taking them to be identified—painstakingly, through dental records and through DNA matches with relatives who were willingly giving their samples to find at least some evidence that their family member had perished that day. The refrigerator trucks were parked near the medical examiner's office. That office was also near Stern College, the Orthodox Jewish college for women that is a larger part of Yeshiva University, the premier Orthodox institution of higher learning in New York City.

When the refrigerator truck was parked there for a day or two, a student from Stern College came out with a small folding chair and sat near the truck. She opened a book and began to sing. Jewish tradition teaches that after someone has died and before the body is buried is a time to honor the person who has left us and acknowledge that his or her remains are still with us. It is part of the tradition of *kevod ha-met*: respect for the body as the vessel that housed the soul in life.[22] During the precious time between death and burial, the body should never be left alone. Jewish communities frequently coordinate this ritual, which is also open to non-Jewish friends and family. It involves sitting with the body of the deceased and chanting the Psalms, reading them quietly, or simply meditating—called the *shmira*, or "guarding" the body.

The women of Stern College knew that the refrigerator truck with the remains of the victims might well contain Jewish remains, so they acted accordingly. Men from a nearby synagogue also joined. Everyone set up chairs and sang the Psalms, performing the shmira. And people gathered. They were not only Jewish people but also secular people, Buddhist people, Muslim people. The women from Stern College did this for entirely Jewish reasons—there could be one Jewish fingernail in that refrigerator truck. As one of the participants put it, they felt joy when the pleas for Sabbath *shomers*, or guardians, came in. "This is something I can do," one participant, Ms. Kaplan said. "And it's surreal. You absolutely feel the souls there, and you feel them feeling better."

But the mourners all around the city needed the women's ritual as well. They needed to guard the remains too, and they saw meaning and purpose and an outlet for their grief and shock in that intensely Jewish ritual, performed by an intensely committed group of Jewish women. In other words, the others gathered round needed Judaism to be itself.

This story is of course moving in its own right—a shared ritual, the possibility of restoring honor and dignity where there was nothing except violence and horror. But it also embodies that second compelling interest: the harmonization of the traditions of religious groups with the ideals of a nation and the broader civic community. In this case that did not mean giving up Jewish identity; it meant engaged with it more fully in the service of the greater good. The greater civic good was the need to mourn, the need to honor, as the Jewish word *kevod* suggests.

And in that moment and space of New York City, there was harmony, and an active working toward harmony, that helped connect the Jewish tradition with the ideals of the nation—ideals that had been so devastatingly shattered. What is more, the greater civic good was also acknowledged by the Orthodox Jewish community's decision to change the gender rules—that men should only sit the shmira for men, and women for women. The authorities felt that the circumstances dictated that that rule could be waived. And Yeshiva University provided security guards for the night shifts. The human need was great. One rabbi called this "loving watching of the corpse a very human act" and noted that the shmira is "the truest and most sublime" of the 613 mitzvahs "because there can never be reciprocity."[23]

Concluding Thoughts

The foregoing stories are not as dramatic as that of the Four Chaplains, which ushered in a new era in the mid-twentieth century in which Jews and Christians were included in the American story. Rather, they are more everyday in nature. In my view, they are all the more powerful for that reason. Situations of pragmatic pluralism are frequently ones of loss and disaster, but they need not be. They can be any situation in which shared human values are communicated through, yet transcend, a religious tradition. They are focused on logistics and not talk: the making of music, the maintenance of bricks and mortar, the proper treatment of the dead. They create a connection among strangers that lasts longer than an episodic conversation.

In addition, they fulfill the basics of a good paradigmatic story. As myths, they are complex and hospitable narratives. And they include in various ways the four elements outlined earlier. First, all the stories invoke a wider sense of a "we"—whether that "we" is the relationship between Jews and Christians as they understand their shared history; Jewish and non-Jewish mourners after 9/11; Reform Jews and Orthodox Jews; Jews, Muslims, and Christians in response to Israeli-Palestinian violence; or Jews and Muslims figuring out what to do after a mosque burns down or after a day at school.

Second, the stories have a particular kind of poetics. Their imagery is compelling, as they include one extraordinary thing in an otherwise ordinary exchange. This could be the exchange between a teacher and a student that causes them suddenly to see each other in new ways. It could be the role of poetry in the mourning of the dead in the midst of a devastated city. It could be the first, and perhaps only, encounter between two rabbis who dislike each other but will help each other nonetheless. It could be a silently shared meal in the midst of outside trouble. Or it could be the rabbi who helps a young woman in a strange country feel at home.

Third, they all have a distinct ethics—a set of paradigmatic actions, which can and should be reflected on. Not all would agree that a Catholic priest should take a class from a Jewish teacher on the history of Western art. But the fact that the student did so creates a moment for reflection. Not all would agree that the shmira rules should be bent for the civic good after 9/11, but the fact that they were made people sit up and notice. Not all would agree that the Reform rabbi should have encouraged the Orthodox congregation to thrive in the same town, given how small the population was. But the relationship was an occasion for reflection. Not all would agree that the interfaith group of women should have kept meeting with each other, given the violent rupture of Jenin. But their decision to do so allowed a new ethics of interfaith engagement to emerge. Not all would agree that the rabbi should have given any space in a synagogue to a Muslim. But his sharing of Jewish space made people wonder what it meant to have a holy space to begin with.

Finally, these stories (we might call them "protomyths") also contain key moments of identity formation. A priest returns to his calling renewed, and a teacher understands herself as more effective than she knew. Young women who did not know what to do after 9/11 suddenly found themselves providing a crucial ritual role for an entire city. Two rabbis acknowledge that their congregational identities depend on each other, against all odds. Members of a women's interfaith group came to understand themselves as interfaith leaders as a result of their perseverance and creativity in maintaining their social network. And an exchange student understands her host country, and the nature of Jews within that country, in a different way, while a Jewish congregation tests its own limits for hospitality and is pleased with the results.

Following Patel's perspective, all of these stories also have something important to say about America. They take place in typical American places: Atlanta; New York City; upstate New York; Victoria, Texas; and Riverdale, New York. These are both urban and rural places, both small and large cities. And even at the most superficial level, they celebrate some possibility of generosity in the midst of difficult circumstances.

But there is something more deeply American about these stories. They just might be the beginning of a new narrative. They are an answer to the question that Patel ends his book by asking: Can we actually tell new stories? They are an answer to Rami Nashashibi's assertion that "it's the new story you tell about America that counts." Like the best myths, they are both complex resources for ongoing reflection and complex calls to ethical action.

Reflecting on these stories, we might ask different kinds of questions about the unique opportunities for pragmatic pluralism. Like the priest at the Breman Museum, might we take a course on a common subject taught by a person of a different faith and see how our perspective will change? James Fredericks, and with him, Francis X. Clooney, talk about having a "secondary" religious tradition that keeps us honest and pushes us to ask questions of ourselves that we might not ask within the confines of our own traditions.[24] Like the women of Stern College, might we make our own mourning rituals also rituals of hospitality, welcoming others so that more people can grieve the loss of the dead with us? Like the two rabbis in upstate New York, might we think about what we share with the members of our religious tradition whom we dislike the most and find a way to reach out to them? Like the Interfaith Sisters of Atlanta, might we think creatively about the ways we can maintain our relationships, even though the conversation on particular topics is going nowhere? Like the rabbi in Riverdale who opens his space to the Indonesian Muslim, have we taken the time to share the buildings of our religious communities with other communities that might need them?

Taking all of these examples of powerful narratives into account, might we reflect anew about how the American situation actually teaches us to be interdependent in new ways? Might we look for ways to develop the everyday interreligious ethics that they depict? We might learn about such ethics from a woman chanting the

Psalms after the disaster of September 2001, but we can take that lesson and plant the seed elsewhere. We can create interdependence in art museums and in kitchens, because theologians, political scientists, and everyday people teach us that these very ordinary but new moments of exchange in fact demonstrate ways of interacting that will prevent violence in the future. They tell a story about a new and old American kind of creativity that involves not simply the single person but also the tiny ways in which groups change relationships—as they protect each other's buildings, provide spaces to pray, mourn each other's dead, and feed each other for the future.

Notes

Introduction

1. Rick Gladstone, "Many Ask, Why Not Call Church Shooting Terrorism?," *New York Times*, June 18, 2015.

2. Sarah Kaplan and Justin Wm. Moyer, "Why Racists Target Black Churches," *Washington Post*, July 1, 2015.

3. Danielle Allen, "Toward a Connected Society," in *Our Compelling Interests: The Value of Diversity for Democracy and a Prosperous Society*, ed. Earl Lewis and Nancy Cantor (Princeton, NJ: Princeton University Press, 2016), 71–105.

4. Rupert W. Nacoste, *Taking on Diversity: How We Can Move from Anxiety to Respect* (Amherst, NY: Prometheus Books, 2015), 160.

5. Michael Walzer, "What Does It Mean to Be an 'American'?," *Social Research* 57, no. 3 (Fall 1990): 591–614.

6. Scott Page, *The Diversity Bonus*, Our Compelling Interests 2 (Princeton, NJ: Princeton University Press, 2017).

7. Allen, "Toward a Connected Society."

8. Diana Eck, *A New Religious America: How a "Christian Country" Has Become the World's Most Religiously Diverse Nation* (San Francisco: Harper, 2001).

9. Latino Jewish Leadership Council, statement at the meeting of the American Jewish Committee, August 21, 2017, Washington, DC.

10. Jim Winkler, "All the President's Preachers," *New York Times*, August 24, 2017.

11. Neeti Upadhye, with contributions from Alan Blinder, "As Jewish Institutions Endure Attacks, Muslims Pledge Financial Aid," *New York Times*, February 28, 2017.

12. Ben Sales, "American Muslims Want to Increase Mosque Security. They're Turning to Jews for Help," Jewish Telegraphic Agency, August 25, 2017, https://www.jta.org/2017/08/25/news-opinion/united-states/american-muslims-want-to-increase-mosque-security-theyre-turning-to-jews-for-help-2.

13. Harry Boyte, "Profile—Augsburg's Paul Pribbenow: On Reweaving the Social Fabric," *Huffington Post*, October 20, 2016.

14. Eboo Patel, *Interfaith Leadership: A Primer* (Boston: Beacon, 2016); Patricia Gurin, Biren Nagda, and Ximena Zúñiga, *Dialogue across Difference: Practice, Theory, and Research on Intergroup Dialogue* (New York: Russell Sage Foundation, 2013).

15. Michiko Kakutani, "Obama's Eulogy, Which Found Its Place in History," *New York Times*, July 3, 2015.

16. Sabrina Tavernise, "A Vandal's Act, Met with Mercy," *New York Times*, August 27, 2017.

17. Maggie Astor and Nicholas Fandos, "Confederate Leaders' Descendants Say Statues Can Come Down," *New York Times*, August 20, 2017.

18. Derek Black, "What White Nationalism Gets Right about American History," *New York Times*, August 19, 2017.

Chapter 1: Religious Diversity and the American Promise

1. Michael Walzer, *What It Means to Be an American* (Venice, Italy: Marsilio, 1992), 53.

2. Ibid., 56.

3. William H. Frey, *Diversity Explosion: How New Racial Demographics Are Remaking America* (Washington, DC: Brookings Institution Press, 2015), 32.

4. *The Papers of George Washington*, Presidential Series, Vol. 6, *1 July 1790–30 November 1790*, ed. Mark A. Mastromarino (Charlottesville: University Press of Virginia, 1996), 284–86.

5. "Transcript of Federalist Papers, No 10 & No. 51 (1787–1788)," accessed March 26, 2018, https://www.ourdocuments.gov/print_friendly.php?flash =false&page=transcript&doc=10&title=Transcript+of+Federalist+Papers%2C +No.+10+%26amp%3B+No.+51+(1787-1788).

6. Quoted in Walter Isaacson, "Citizen Ben's 7 Great Virtues," *Time Magazine*, July 17, 2003, http://content.time.com/time/magazine/article/0,9171,1005149 -12,00.html.

7. Denise Spellberg, *Thomas Jefferson's Qur'an: Islam and the Founders* (New York: Vintage Books, 2013), 197.

8. Jonathan A. Wright, *Shapers of the Great Debate on the Freedom of Religion* (Westport, CT: Greenwood, 2005), 42.

9. Michael W. Kaufmann, *Institutional Individualism* (Hanover, NH: Wesleyan University Press, 1998), 71.

10. Macon Phillips, "President Barack Obama's Inaugural Address," January 21, 2009, the White House, https://obamawhitehouse.archives.gov/blog/2009/01 /21/president-barack-obamas-inaugural-address.

11. Glenn Beck and Kevin Balfe, *An Inconvenient Book* (New York: Simon & Schuster, 2007), 146.

12. Quoted in Rachel Swarns, "Congressman Criticizes Election of Muslim," *New York Times*, December 21, 2006.

13. Su'ad Abdul Khabeer, *Muslim Cool: Race, Religion, and Hip Hop in the United States* (New York: New York University Press, 2016), 8.

14. Dalia Mogahed and Youssef Chouhoud, *American Muslim Poll 2017: Muslims at the Crossroads* (Dearborn, MI: Institute for Social Policy and Understanding, 2017).

15. Keith Ellison, *My Country, Tis of Thee: My Faith, My Family, Our Future* (New York: Gallery Books/Karen Hunter, 2014), 224.

16. Ibid.

17. Spellberg, *Thomas Jefferson's Qur'an.*

18. Ibid., 4.

19. Earl Lewis and Nancy Cantor, introduction to *Our Compelling Interests: The Value of Diversity for Democracy and a Prosperous Society*, ed. Earl Lewis and Nancy Cantor (Princeton, NJ: Princeton University Press, 2016), 11.

20. Ibid., 41.

21. "Muslim Americans: Middle Class and Mostly Mainstream," Pew Research Center, May 22, 2007, http://www.pewresearch.org/2007/05/22/muslim-ameri cans-middle-class-and-mostly-mainstream/.

22. Holly Yan, "The Truth about Muslims in America," CNN, December 9, 2015, http://www.cnn.com/2015/12/08/us/muslims-in-america-shattering -misperception/index.html.

23. Caryle Murphy, "The Most and Least Educated U.S. Religious Groups," *Fact Tank*, Pew Research Center, November 4, 2016, http://www.pewresearch.org /fact-tank/2016/11/04/the-most-and-least-educated-u-s-religious-groups/.

24. George Washington Society, "The Bosom of America," accessed March 26, 2018, https://waquote.wordpress.com/2012/02/20/the-bosom-of-america/.

25. Alexis de Tocqueville, *Democracy in America*, quoted by Foundation Tocqueville 2018, accessed March 26, 2018, http://tocquevillefoundation.org /overview/.

26. Ibid.

27. Robert Putnam, *Bowling Alone: The Collapse and Revival of American Community* (New York: Simon and Schuster, 2000), 66.

28. Robert Putnam and David Campbell, *American Grace: How Religion Divides and Unites Us* (New York: Simon and Schuster, 2012), 454.

29. John Rawls, *The Law of Peoples with "The Idea of Public Reason Revisited"* (Cambridge, MA: Harvard University Press, March 2001).

30. Stephen Prothero, *God Is Not One: The Eight Rival Religions That Run the World* (New York: Harper One, 2001), 2.

31. Robert Putnam, "*E Pluribus Unum*: Diversity and Community in the 21st Century: The 2006 Johan Skytte Prize Lecture," *Scandinavian Political Studies* 30, no. 2 (June 2007): 137–74.

32. Christian Smith and Melinda Lundquist Denton, *Soul Searching: The Religious and Spiritual Life of American Teenagers* (New York: Oxford University Press, 2005).

33. Peter Berger, *The Heretical Imperative: Contemporary Possibilities of Religious Affirmation* (New York: Doubleday, 1980), 17.

34. Ibid., 17.

35. Ibid., 23.

36. Peter Berger, "The Good of Religious Pluralism," *First Things*, April 2016, https://www.firstthings.com/article/2016/04/the-good-of-religious-pluralism.

37. Ibid.

38. Diana L. Eck, "What is Pluralism?," The Pluralism Project, Harvard University, 2006, http://pluralism.org/what-is-pluralism/.

39. Walzer, *What It Means*, 15

40. Eboo Patel, *Interfaith Leadership: A Primer* (Boston: Beacon, 2016).

41. Danielle Allen, "Toward a Connected Society," in Lewis and Cantor, *Our Compelling Interests*, 90.

42. Donald R. McClarey, "George Washington and Catholics," American Catholic, November 5, 2009, https://the-american-catholic.com/2009/11/05/george-washington-and-catholics/.

43. Spellberg, *Thomas Jefferson's Qur'an*, 81.

44. Putnam and Campbell, *American Grace*.

45. Ibid., 516.

46. Ashutosh Varshney, *Ethnic Conflict and Civic Life* (New Haven, CT: Yale University Press, 2002).

47. Philip Gorski, *American Covenant: A History of Civil Religion from the Puritans to the Present* (Princeton, NJ: Princeton University Press, 2017), 4.

48. Ibid., 16.

49. Ibid., 17.

50. Quoted in Martin E. Marty, *The One and the Many: America's Struggle for the Common Good* (Cambridge, MA: Harvard University Press, 1997), 140.

51. Walter Lippmann, *Public Opinion* (New York: Harcourt, Brace, 1922), 25.

52. Quoted in Marty, *The One and the Many*, 9.

53. George Washington, "Letter to the Roman Catholics," March 15, 1790, http://teachingamericanhistory.org/library/document/letter-to-the-roman-catholics/.

54. Marty, *The One and the Many*.

55. Ibid., 145.

56. Jeffrey Stout, *Democracy and Tradition* (Princeton NJ: Princeton University Press, 2004), 298.

57. Linda Chavez, "What Trump Can Learn from a Gold Star Family," *New York Times*, October 20, 2017.

58. Allen, "Toward a Connected Society"; Patricia Gurin, "Group Interactions in Building a Connected Society," in Lewis and Cantor, *Our Compelling Interests*, 170–81.

Chapter 2: Cordoba House

Eboo Patel, *Sacred Ground: Pluralism, Prejudice, and the Promise of America* (Boston: Beacon, 2012). Reprinted by permission of Beacon Press, Boston.

1. Ralph Blumenthal and Sharaf Mowjood, "Muslim Prayers and Renewal Near Ground Zero," *New York Times*, December 8, 2009.

2. Quoted in Maria Rosa Menocal, *Ornament of the World: How Muslims, Jews and Christians Created a Culture of Tolerance in Medieval Spain* (Boston: Little, Brown, 2002), 32.

3. Feisal Abdul Rauf, *What's Right with Islam Is What's Right with America: A New Vision for Muslims and the West* (New York: HarperCollins, 2005).

4. Pamela Geller, "Mosque at Ground Zero: Adding Insult to Agony," *Geller Report*, December 11, 2017, https://pamelageller.com/2009/12/mosque-at -ground-zero-adding-insult-to-agony.html/.

5. Bobby Ghosh/Dearborn, "Islamophobia: Does America Have a Muslim Problem?," in "Is America Islamophobic?," special issue, *Time Magazine*, August 30, 2010.

6. Quoted in Andy Barr, "Newt Compares Mosque to Nazis," *Politico Magazine*, August 16, 2010, https://www.politico.com/story/2010/08/newt-compares -mosque-to-nazis-041112.

7. Quoted in Howard Kurtz, "Making of a Mosque Mess," *Washington Post*, August 17, 2010, http://www.washingtonpost.com/wp-dyn/content/article /2010/08/17/AR2010081701473.html.

8. Quoted in Scott Shane, "In Islamic Law, Gingrich Sees a Mortal Threat to the U.S.," *New York Times*, December 21, 2011.

9. Frank Gaffney, *Sharia: The Threat to America* (Washington, DC: Center for Security Policy, October 2010), 222.

10. Michael R. Bloomberg, "Defending Religious Tolerance: Remarks on the Mosque Near Ground Zero," *Huffington Post*, August 3, 2010, https://www .huffingtonpost.com/michael-bloomberg/mayor-bloomberg-on-the-ne_b _669338.html.

Chapter 3: The Islamophobia Industry in the White House

1. Quoted in Nadia Marzouki, *Islam: An American Religion*, trans. Christopher Jon Delogu (New York: Columbia University Press, 2017), 199.

2. Frank Gaffney, *Sharia: The Threat to America* (Washington, DC: Center for Security Policy, October 2010).

3. The Tiger Team, "The Secure Freedom Strategy: A Plan for Victory over the Global Jihad Movement," January 23, 2015, 15, https://www .centerforsecuritypolicy.org/wp-content/uploads/2015/01/Secure_Freedom _Strategy_01-23-15.pdf.

4. Peter Beinart, "The Denationalization of American Muslims," *Atlantic*, March 19, 2017.

5. Peter Beinart, "Trump's Anti-Muslim Political Strategy," *Atlantic*, November 29, 2017, https://www.theatlantic.com/politics/archive/2017/11/trumps -anti-muslim-retweets-shouldnt-surprise-you/547031/?utm_source=nl-atlantic -daily-112917&silverid=MzEwMTkwMTQ5MDA2S0.

6. Jenna Johnson and Abigail Hauslohner, "'I Think Islam Hates Us': A Timeline of Trump's Comments about Islam and Muslims," *Washington Post*, May 20, 2017, https://www.washingtonpost.com/news/post-politics/wp/2017 /05/20/i-think-islam-hates-us-a-timeline-of-trumps-comments-about-islam-and -muslims/?utm_term=.119c7bf52944; Philip Bump, "Meet Frank Gaffney, the

Anti-Muslim Gadfly Reportedly Advising Donald Trump's Transition Team," *Washington Post*, November 16, 2016, https://www.washingtonpost.com/news /the-fix/wp/2015/12/08/meet-frank-gaffney-the-anti-muslim-gadfly-who -produced-donald-trumps-anti-muslim-poll/?utm_term=.0cf106656707.

7. Daniel Kahneman, *Thinking, Fast and Slow* (New York: Farrar, Straus and Giroux, 2011).

8. "Full: Second Presidential Debate—Donald Trump vs. Hillary Clinton— Washington University, 10/9/2016," YouTube, minute 33:45, NBC News, https:// www.youtube.com/watch?v=FRlI2SQ0Ueg.

9. Janelle Ross, "A Muslim Woman Asked Trump How He'd Battle Islamophobia. He Decided to Answer a Different Question," *Washington Post*, October 9, 2016.

10. Johnson and Hauslohner, "'I Think Islam Hates Us.'"

11. Nicholas Kristof, "Husbands Are Deadlier Than Terrorists," *New York Times*, February 11, 2017.

12. Alexandra King, "Fareed Zakaria: Victims of Travel Ban the 'Roadkill of Trump's Posturing,'" CNN, January 30, 2017, https://www.cnn.com/2017/01/29 /us/zakaria-take-executive-order-cnntv/index.html.

13. Farhana Khera and Johnathan J. Smith, "How Trump Is Stealthily Carrying Out His Muslim Ban," *New York Times*, July 18, 2007, https://www.nytimes.com /2017/07/18/opinion/trump-muslim-ban-supreme-court.html?_r=0.

14. Scott Shane and Matthew Rosenberg, "Trump Pushes Dark View of Islam to Center of U.S. Policy-Making," *New York Times*, February 1, 2017, https://www .nytimes.com/2017/02/01/us/politics/donald-trump-islam.html?_r=0.

15. Thomas Gibbons-Neff, "'Fear of Muslims is Rational': What Trump's New National Security Adviser Has Said Online," *Washington Post*, November 18, 2016, https://www.washingtonpost.com/news/checkpoint/wp/2016/11/18/trumps -new-national-security-adviser-has-said-some-incendiary-things-on-the-internet /?utm_term=.db3b6c982302.

16. SPLC (Southern Poverty Law center), "ACT for America," https://www .splcenter.org/fighting-hate/extremist-files/group/act-america.

17. Mark Landler and Eric Schmitt, "H. R. McMaster Breaks with Administration on Views of Islam," *New York Times*, February 24, 2017.

18. Peter Beinart, "The U.S. Government's Fight against Violent Extremism Loses Its Leader," *Atlantic*, July 31, 2017.

19. Joshua Green, *Devil's Bargain: Steve Bannon, Donald Trump, and the Storming of the Presidency* (New York: Penguin, 2017).

20. Christopher Caldwell, *Reflections on the Revolution in Europe: Immigration, Islam, and the West* (New York: Doubleday, July 2009).

21. Christopher Caldwell, "What Does Steve Bannon Want?," *New York Times*, February 25, 2017, https://www.nytimes.com/2017/02/25/opinion/what-does -steve-bannon-want.html.

22. Matea Gold, "Bannon Film Outline Warned U.S. Could Turn into 'Islamic States of America,'" *Washington Post*, February 3, 2017.

23. Olga Khazan, "The Dark Minds of the 'Alt-Right,'" *Atlantic*, August 17, 2017.

24. Jonathan Capehart, "Trump's Horrible and Predictable Response to White Supremacy in Charlottesville," *Washington Post*, August 14, 2017, https://www.washingtonpost.com/blogs/post-partisan/wp/2017/08/14/trumps-horrible-and-predictable-response-to-white-supremacy-in-charlottesville/?utm_term=.a6db6c3e3c19.

25. Dana Milbank, "Trump Just Hit a New Low," *Washington Post*, August 15, 2017, https://www.washingtonpost.com/opinions/its-looking-more-and-more-like-the-white-nationalist-house/2017/08/15/eb5828b4-81fb-11e7-ab27-1a21a8e006ab_story.html?utm_term=.f309a3f9a8c1.

26. Associated Press, "Portland Stabbing Suspect: 'You Call It Terrorism, I Call It Patriotism!,'" *Politico*, May 30, 2017, https://www.politico.com/story/2017/05/30/portland-attacks-muslims-bias-238955.

27. Holly Yan and Mayra Curevas, "Spate of Mosque Fires Stretches across the Country," CNN, March 2, 2017, https://www.cnn.com/2017/03/02/us/mosque-fires-2017/index.html.

28. Nancy Coleman, "On Average, 9 Mosques Have Been Targeted Every Month This Year," CNN, August 7, 2017, http://www.cnn.com/2017/03/20/us/mosques-targeted-2017-trnd/index.html.

29. Lois Beckett, "Anti-Muslim Hate Groups Nearly Triple in US since Last Year, Report Finds," *Guardian*, February 15, 2017, https://www.theguardian.com/us-news/2017/feb/15/anti-muslim-hate-groups-increase-far-right-neo-nazis.

30. Ibid.

31. Maria Konnikova, "How Norms Change," *New Yorker*, October 11, 2017, https://www.newyorker.com/science/maria-konnikova/how-norms-change.

32. David A. Graham, "The Panic President," *Atlantic*, June 4, 2017, https://www.theatlantic.com/politics/archive/2017/06/donald-trump-sadiq-khan/529110.

33. Elliot Hannon, "Gunman Charged with Deadly Quebec City Mosque Mass Shooting Appears to Be a White Nationalist," *Slate*, January 30, 2017, http://www.slate.com/blogs/the_slatest/2017/01/30/deadly_quebec_city_mosque_shooter_appears_to_be_a_white_nationalist.html.

34. "Trump Speaks at MacDill Air Force Base, Florida—Full Speech," YouTube, posted by Michael McIntee on February 6, 2017, https://www.youtube.com/watch?v=d10teC1E-a4.

35. Associated Press, "WH Releases List of Terror Attacks It Claims Didn't Get Enough Coverage," CBS News, February 7, 2017, www.cbsnews.com/news/white-house-releases-list-of-terror-attacks-says-most-didnt-receive-media-attention-they-deserved/.

36. Katie Mettler and Derek Hawkins, "What's Largely and Glaringly Missing from Trump's List of Terrorist Attacks: Non-Western Victims," *New York Times*, February 7, 2017.

37. Jelani Cobb, "Inside the Trial of Dylann Roof," *New Yorker*, February 6, 2017.

38. Aaron Blake, "Kellyanne Conway's 'Bowling Green Massacre' Wasn't a Slip of the Tongue. She Has Said It Before," *Washington Post*, February 6, 2017, https://www.washingtonpost.com/news/the-fix/wp/2017/02/06/kellyanne-conways-bowling-green-massacre-wasnt-a-slip-of-the-tongue-shes-said-it-before/?utm_term=.e3596ead994b.

39. A. C. Thompson, "When We Really Did Fear a Bowling Green Massacre," *New York Times*, February 8, 2017.

40. Ibid.

41. Ron Nixon and Eileen Sullivan, "Revocation of Grants to Help Fight Hate under New Scrutiny after Charlottesville," *New York Times*, August 15, 2017.

42. "Text: Obama's Speech in Cairo," *New York Times*, June 4, 2009, http://www.nytimes.com/2009/06/04/us/politics/04obama.text.html?mtrref=www.google.com.

43. Jennifer Gonnerman, "A Syrian Doctor Returns to Illinois," *New Yorker*, February 2, 2017.

44. Donald G. McNeil Jr., "Trump's Travel Ban, Aimed at Terrorists, Has Blocked Doctors," *New York Times*, February 6, 2017.

45. Julia Preston, "Ailing Midwestern Cities Extend a Welcoming Hand to Immigrants," *New York Times*, October 6, 2013.

46. Jess Bidgood, "Ailing Vermont Town Pins Hopes on Mideast Refugees," *New York Times*, January 2, 2017.

47. Eric Posner, "Judges v. Trump: Be Careful What You Wish For," *New York Times*, February 15, 2017.

48. Noah Feldman, "Court Essentially Says Trump Lied about Travel Ban," Bloomberg, May 25, 2017, https://www.bloomberg.com/view/articles/2017-05-25/court-essentially-says-trump-lied-about-travel-ban?utm_medium=email&utm_source=newsletter&utm_term=170526&utm_campaign=sharetheview.

49. Vikki Ortiz Healy, "The Story behind the Viral Photo of Muslim and Jewish Children Protesting at O'Hare," *Chicago Tribune*, February 1, 2017, http://www.chicagotribune.com/news/local/breaking/ct-jewish-muslim-fathers-viral-photo-met-20170131-story.html.

50. Laurie Goodstein, "Both Feeling Threatened, American Muslims and Jews Join Hands," *New York Times*, December 5, 2016, https://www.nytimes.com/2016/12/05/us/muslim-jewish-alliance-after-trump.html.

51. "#NeverIsNow: Opening Remarks by ADL CEO Jonathan Greenblatt," given at the Anti-Defamation League's "Never Is Now" Summit on Anti-Semitism, New York City, November 17, 2016, https://www.adl.org/blog/neverisnow-opening-remarks-by-adl-ceo-jonathan-greenblatt.

52. Tarek El-Messidi, "News just broke earlier today that another Jewish cemetery was vandalized—this time in Philadelphia (where I currently live)," Facebook, February 26, 2017, https://www.facebook.com/elmessidi/videos/10104721332733245/?fallback=1.

53. Yonat Shimron, "Meet the Only Imam to Pray before Congress Twice," *Sojourners*, October 5, 2017, https://sojo.net/articles/meet-only-imam-pray-congress-twice.

Chapter 4: Toward an Interfaith America

1. Peter Beinart, "The Denationalization of American Muslims," *Atlantic*, March 19, 2017.

2. Quoted in Kevin M. Schultz, *Tri-faith America: How Catholics and Jews Held Postwar America to Its Protestant Promise* (New York: Oxford University Press, 2011), 19.

3. Beinart, "Denationalization of American Muslims."

4. Schultz, *Tri-faith America*, 33.

5. Maria Monk, *Awful Disclosures by Maria Monk of the Hotel Dieu Nunnery of Montreal* (Whitefish, MT: Kessinger, 2003).

6. Fintan O'Toole, "Green Beer and Rank Hypocrisy," *New York Times*, March 16, 2017.

7. Scott Shane, "Stephen Bannon in 2014: We Are at War with Radical Islam," *New York Times*, February 1, 2017.

8. Quoted in Schultz, *Tri-faith America*, 10.

9. Richard Bulliet, *The Case for Islamo-Christian Civilization* (New York: Columbia University Press, 2004), 10,

10. Schultz, *Tri-faith America*, 45.

11. Quoted in ibid., 52.

12. Schultz, *Tri-faith America*, 51.

13. Robert Putnam and David Campbell, *American Grace: How Religion Divides and Unites Us* (New York: Simon and Schuster, 2012).

14. Dennis Prager, "What Does 'Judeo-Christian' Mean?," Dennis Prager Show, March 30, 2004, http://www.dennisprager.com/what-does-judeo-christian-mean/.

15. Bulliet, *Case for Islamo-Christian Civilization*, 41–42.

16. Dan Merica, "Trump: 'We Are Stopping Cold the Attacks on Judeo-Christian Values,'" CNN Politics, October 13, 2017, https://www.cnn.com/2017/10/13/politics/trump-values-voters-summit/index.html.

17. Bulliet, *Case for Islamo-Christian Civilization*, 38.

18. Anand Giridharadas, *The True American: Murder and Mercy in Texas* (New York: W. W. Norton, 2014).

19. Sharon Otterman, "Obscuring a Muslim Name, and an American's Sacrifice," *New York Times*, January 1, 2012, http://www.nytimes.com/2012/01/02/nyregion/sept-11-memorial-obscures-a-police-cadets-bravery.html?mcubz=0.

20. Krishnadev Calamur, "Muhammad Ali and Vietnam," *Atlantic*, June 4, 2016, https://www.theatlantic.com/news/archive/2016/06/muhammad-ali-vietnam/485717/.

21. Cindy Boren, "The Iconic Moment Muhammad Ali Lit Olympic Flame in Atlanta Almost Didn't Happen," *Washington Post*, June 4, 2016, https://www .washingtonpost.com/news/early-lead/wp/2016/06/04/the-iconic-moment -muhammad-ali-lit-olympic-torch-in-atlanta-almost-didnt-happen/?utm_term =.8ab6320e8bd9.

22. Krishnadev Calamur, "Muhammad Ali and Vietnam," *Atlantic*, June 4, 2016, https://www.theatlantic.com/news/archive/2016/06/muhammad-ali -vietnam/485717/.

23. Arnie Seipel, "READ: President Obama's Remembrance Of Muhammad Ali," NPR, June 4, 2016, https://www.npr.org/2016/06/04/480743833/read -president-obamas-remembrance-of-muhammad-ali.

Chapter 5: The American *Ummah* in the Era of Islamophobia

1. Karen Swallow Prior, "Why Walt Whitman Called America the 'Greatest Poem,'" *Atlantic*, December 25, 2016, https://www.theatlantic.com/entertain ment/archive/2016/12/why-walt-whitman-called-the-america-the-greatest -poem/510932/.

2. Chaim Potok, *The Chosen* (New York: Ballantine Books, 1967).

3. Aziz Ansari, "Aziz Ansari: Why Trump Makes Me Scared for My Family," op-ed, *New York Times*, June 24, 2016.

4. *Master of None*, season 2, episode 3, "Religion," directed by Alan Yang, written by Aziz Ansari, May 12, 2017, Netflix.

5. After I completed this manuscript, a story emerged about Aziz Ansari's sexual aggressiveness during a date that raises troubling questions about not just what sort of Muslim he is, but what sort of person. Stories of a more serious sort have emerged with respect to Leon Wieseltier, who I also quote. Where their work is useful, we should engage with it, as I do here. And where their behavior crosses lines of decency and causes pain, we should note it, as I am doing now. See https://www.cnn.com/2018/01/15/entertainment/aziz-ansari-responds /ind and https://www.vox.com/first-person/2017/11/9/16624588/new -republic-hara.

6. Leon Wieseltier, "The Catastrophist," review of *The Second Plane*, by Martin Amis, *New York Times*, April 27, 2008, Sunday Book Review.

7. Kelefa Sanneh, "Funny Person—Can a Hardworking Cult Favorite Make It as a Mainstream Star?," *New Yorker*, November 1, 2010.

8. Zahra Noorbaksh, "After Trump's Election, a Nonpracticing Muslim Returns to Prayer," *Fresh Air*, NPR, January 18, 2017, https://www.npr.org/2017/01/18 /510346895/after-trumps-election-a-non-practicing-muslim-returns-to-prayer.

9. Noah Berlatsky, "What Makes the Muslim Ms. Marvel Awesome: She's Just like Everyone," *Atlantic*, March 20, 2014.

10. Alan Feuer, "Linda Sarsour Is a Brooklyn Homegirl in a Hijab," *New York Times*, August 7, 2015, https://www.nytimes.com/2015/08/09/nyregion/linda -sarsour-is-a-brooklyn-homegirl-in-a-hijab.html?_r=0.

11. Atossa Abrahamian, "Who's Afraid of Linda Sarsour?," *Fader*, Fall 2017, http://www.thefader.com/2017/04/27/linda-sarsour-interview-feminism-sharia-womens-march.

12. Eli Rosenberg, "A Muslim-American Activist's Speech Raises Ire Even before It's Delivered," *New York Times*, May 26, 2017, https://www.nytimes.com/2017/05/26/nyregion/linda-sarsour-cuny-speech-protests.html.

13. Time Staff, "Linda Sarsour Gives CUNY Commencement Speech: 'Commit to Never Being Bystanders,'" *Time Magazine*, June 2, 2017, http://time.com/4802373/linda-sarsour-cuny-commencement-address-transcript/.

14. "Islamic Teachings on Abortion," Religions, BBC, September 7, 2009, http://www.bbc.co.uk/religion/religions/islam/islamethics/abortion_1.shtml.

15. Ali Gharib, "Muslim, American, & Intersectional: The Activism of Linda Sarsour," *ACLU Blog*, August 22, 2016, https://www.aclu.org/blog/immigrants-rights/muslim-american-intersectional-activism-linda-sarsour.

16. "Religious Freedom: Why Now? A Conversation on Islam and Religious Freedom with Dr. Robert P. George and Shaykh Hamza Yusuf," Religious Freedom Project, Berkley Center for Religion Peace & World Affairs, March 1, 2012, https://berkleycenter.georgetown.edu/publications/religious-freedom-why-now-a-conversation-on-islam-and-religious-freedom-with-dr-robert-p-george-and-shaykh-hamza-yusuf.

17. Peter Manseau, *One Nation, under Gods: A New American History* (New York: Back Bay Books, 2017), 404.

18. Ibid., 59.

19. Ibid.

20. Ibid., 63.

21. Negin Farsad and Dean Obeidallah, dirs., *The Muslims Are Coming!* (New York: Vaguely Qualified Productions/Filmbuff, 2013).

22. Sarah Harvard, "Why Doesn't the Muslim Community Look Up to Its Black Celebrities?," *Washington Post*, September 20, 2017, https://www.washingtonpost.com/news/acts-of-faith/wp/2017/09/20/why-doesnt-the-muslim-community-look-up-to-its-black-celebrities/?utm_term=.ac77b782c261.

23. Ibid.

Chapter 6: IMAN

1. Su'ad Abdul Khabeer, *Muslim Cool: Race, Religion, and Hip Hop in the United States* (New York: New York University Press, 2016), 8, 13.

2. Personal conversation with author, August 1, 2017, Chicago.

3. Quoted in Diana Eck, *A New Religious America: How a "Christian Country" Has Become the World's Most Religiously Diverse Nation* (New York: HarperCollins, 2001), 7.

4. Kevin M. Schultz, *Tri-faith America: How Catholics and Jews Held Postwar America to Its Protestant Promise* (New York: Oxford University Press, 2011).

5. Dr. Umar Faruq Abd-Allah, "Islam and the Cultural Imperative: A Nawawi Foundation Paper" (Nawawi Foundation, 2004), 1, http://www.artsrn .ualberta.ca/amcdouga/Hist347/additional%20rdgs/article%20culture%20 imperative.pdf.

Chapter 7: Postscript

1. Michael Showalter, dir., *The Big Sick* (Santa Monica, CA: Lions Gate Entertainment, 2017).

2. Nadia Marzouki, *Islam: An American Religion*, trans. Christopher Jon Delogu (New York: Columbia University Press, 2017), 21.

3. "Hasan Minhaj: *Homecoming King* (2017)—Full Transcript," Scraps from the Loft, October 21, 2017, http://scrapsfromtheloft.com/2017/10/21/hasan -minhaj-homecoming-king-2017-full-transcript/.

Chapter 8: The Challenge of Pluralism after the End of White Christian America

1. Will Herberg, *Protestant, Catholic, Jew: An Essay in American Religious Sociology* (Chicago: University of Chicago Press, 1983; originally published 1955).

2. Robert P. Jones, *The End of White Christian America* (New York: Simon and Schuster, 2016).

3. Ibid.

4. Robert P. Jones and Daniel Cox, *America's Changing Religious Identity: Findings from the 2016 American Values Atlas* (Washington, DC: PRRI, 2017), https://www.prri.org/research/american-religious-landscape-christian -religiously-unaffiliated/.

5. Ibid.; Tom W. Smith, Peter Marsden, Michael Hout, and Jibum Kim, *General Social Surveys, 1972–2014* [machine-readable data file] (Chicago: NORC at the University of Chicago, 2015).

6. Jones and Cox, *America's Changing Religious Identity*.

7. Michael Hout, Andrew Greeley, and Melissa J. Wilde, "The Demographic Imperative in Religious Change in the United States," *American Journal of Sociology* 107, no. 2 (September 2001): 468–500.

8. Smith et al., *General Social Surveys*.
Note: It is not possible to distinguish between evangelical and mainline Protestants in the 1976 General Social Survey, but the median age of white Protestants overall is significantly lower than that of either group today.

9. Jones and Cox, *America's Changing Religious Identity*.

10. Ibid.; Allison Pond, Gregory Smith, and Scott Clement, "Religion among the Millennials," Pew Research Center, February 17, 2010, http://www.pewforum .org/2010/02/17/religion-among-the-millennials/.

11. Robert P. Jones, Daniel Cox, Betsy Cooper, and Rachel Lienesch, *Exodus: Why Americans Are Leaving Religion—and Why They're Unlikely to Come Back*

(Washington, DC: PRRI and Religion News Service, 2016), http://www.prri.org /research/prri-rns-poll-nones-atheist-leaving-religion/.

12. Robert Putnam and David Campbell, *American Grace: How Religion Unites and Divides Us* (New York: Simon and Schuster, 2010), 141.

13. Conrad Hackett, "5 Facts about the Muslim Population in Europe," Pew Research Center, 2017, http://www.pewresearch.org/fact-tank/2016/07/19/5 -facts-about-the-muslim-population-in-europe/.

14. Michael Lipka, "Muslims and Islam: Key Findings in the U.S. and around the World," Pew Research Center, August 9, 2017, http://www.pewresearch.org /fact-tank/2017/08/09/muslims-and-islam-key-findings-in-the-u-s-and-around -the-world/.

15. Robert P. Jones, Daniel Cox, Betsy Cooper, and Rachel Lienesch, *Beyond Economics: Fears of Cultural Displacement Pushed the White Working Class to Trump* (Washington, DC: PRRI, 2017), https://www.prri.org/research/white-working -class-attitudes-economy-trade-immigration-election-donald-trump/.

16. Merle Black and Earl Black, *The Rise of Southern Republicans* (Cambridge, MA: Harvard University Press, 2003), 4.

17. Portions of this section have been adapted from my op-ed published in the *New York Times*. See Robert P. Jones, "The Collapse of American Identity," *New York Times*, May 4, 2017.

18. Jones and Cox, *America's Changing Religious Identity*.

19. Associated Press and NORC Center for Public Affairs Research, "The American Identity: Points of Pride, Conflicting Views, and a Distinct Culture," AP-NORC, 2017, http://apnorc.org/projects/Pages/HTML%20Reports/points -of-pride-conflicting-views-and-a-distinct-culture.aspx. Note that the original AP-NORC report includes independents who lean toward the Republican Party in their breakouts of "Republicans" in their report. I have rerun the analysis to exclude leaners from my definition of "Republican" to be consistent with other findings.

20. Robert P. Jones and Daniel Cox, *Majority of Americans Oppose Transgender Bathroom Restrictions* (Washington, DC: PRRI, 2017), https://www.prri.org /research/lgbt-transgender-bathroom-discrimination-religious-liberty/.

21. Not wanting to reinforce the patriarchal assumptions built into our dining set, our family has chosen to give that seat to our daughter.

22. G. K. Chesterton, *What I Saw in America* (Edinburgh: Edinburgh University Press, 1922).

23. Ibid., 7.

24. Jones et al., *Exodus*.

25. Ibid.

26. Jeffrey Stout, *Ethics after Babel: The Languages of Morals and Their Discontents* (Princeton, NJ: Princeton University Press, 2001), 292.

27. Steven Tipton, *Public Pulpits: Methodists and Mainline Churches in the Moral Argument of Public Life* (Chicago: University of Chicago Press, 2008), 39.

Chapter 9: Hope without a Common Good

1. John D. Inazu, *Confident Pluralism: Surviving and Thriving through Deep Difference* (Chicago: University of Chicago Press, 2016).

2. Rod Dreher, "Training for the Resistance," *American Conservative*, May 31, 2016.

3. Paul Horwitz, "Positive Pluralism Now," *University of Chicago Law Review* 84 (2017): 1019 (review of *Confident Pluralism*).

4. Carl Trueman, "Confident Pluralism Indeed," *First Things*, May 27, 2016 (review of *Confident Pluralism*), https://www.firstthings.com/blogs/firstthoughts /2016/05/confident-pluralism-indeed.

5. Gene Zubovich, "The Strange, Short Career of Judeo-Christianity," *Aeon*, March 22, 2016. Zubovich observes that "the phrase 'Judeo-Christian' first became popular in the late 1930s, when President Franklin Roosevelt began trying to mobilize Americans against Nazism."

6. Will Herberg, *Protestant, Catholic, Jew: An Essay in American Religious Sociology* (Garden City, NY: Doubleday, 1955).

7. Zubovich, "Strange, Short Career."

8. Ibid. Here, Zubovich's account is oversimplified. For example, he omits the reasons that Catholics and Jews also moved toward a broader ecumenical partnership, with the former including Vatican II in 1959 and the underlying influence of John Courtney Murray. See John Courtney Murray, *We Hold These Truths: Catholic Reflections on the American Proposition* (New York: Sheed and Ward, 1960). Zubovich also suggests that conservative Protestants moved en masse toward an embrace of Judeo-Christianity in the 1960s. But the Supreme Court's school prayer decisions in 1962 and 1963 prompted another push for the Christian amendment, and it was proposed as late as 1984. Today, some conservative Protestants still reject partnerships with Catholics and Jews, and others argue that the United States has always been and should always be a "Christian nation." See, e.g., David Barton, *Original Intent: The Courts, the Constitution, and Religion* (Aledo, TX: WallBuilder, 1996); Tim LaHaye, *Faith of Our Founding Fathers* (Brentwood, TN: Wolgemunt and Hyatt, 1987); and Jerry Falwell, *Listen, America!* (New York: Bantam Books, 1981). For a critique of these kinds of accounts, see John Fea, *Was America Founded as a Christian Nation? A Historical Introduction* (Louisville, KY: Westminster John Knox, 2011).

9. See, e.g., Kimberly Winston, "Poll Shows Atheism on the Rise in the U.S.," *Washington Post*, August 13, 2012 (noting that in a recent worldwide poll on religiosity and atheism, "the number of Americans who say they are atheists rose, from 1 percent to 5 percent"); and Daniel Cox, "Way More Americans May Be Atheists than We Thought," *FiveThirtyEight*, May 18, 2017 (reporting on a study suggesting that the number of atheists in the United States may be up to ten times higher than previously estimated).

10. 572 U.S. ___ (2014).

11. Ibid.

12. Ibid.

13. Ibid. The Court relied on an earlier decision, *Marsh v. Chambers*, 463 U.S. 783 (1983). *Marsh* addressed the practice of the Nebraska legislature of opening each legislative day with a prayer by a chaplain who was paid by the state. The Court concluded that long-standing historical practice in the United States (including in the United States Congress) suggested that legislative prayer did not violate the First Amendment's Establishment Clause. The Court further entrenched these principles in *Greece*:

> *Marsh* must not be understood as permitting a practice that would amount to a constitutional violation if not for its historical foundation. The case teaches instead that the Establishment Clause must be interpreted "by reference to historical practices and understandings." That the First Congress provided for the appointment of chaplains only days after approving language for the First Amendment demonstrates that the Framers considered legislative prayer a benign acknowledgment of religion's role in society. In the 1850's, the judiciary committees in both the House and Senate reevaluated the practice of official chaplaincies after receiving petitions to abolish the office. The committees concluded that the office posed no threat of an establishment because lawmakers were not compelled to attend the daily prayer, no faith was excluded by law, nor any favored; and the cost of the chaplain's salary imposed a vanishingly small burden on taxpayers. *Marsh* stands for the proposition that it is not necessary to define the precise boundary of the Establishment Clause where history shows that the specific practice is permitted. (*Town of Greece*, 572 U.S. at ____)

14. *Town of Greece*, 572 U.S. at ____.

15. Ibid., ____ (Kagan, J., dissenting).

16. Ibid.

17. Ibid.

18. Steven D. Smith, "Discourse in the Dusk: The Twilight of Religious Freedom?," *Harvard Law Review* 122 (2009): 1884 (entertaining the possibility that while "religious speech, practice, and association might still enjoy substantial protection under other constitutional provisions and principles—free speech, perhaps, or equal protection," there may be "no good justification for treating religion as a special legal category").

19. These kinds of questions also highlight the difficulty of defining the term *religion* for constitutional or statutory purposes. See, e.g., George C. Freeman III, "The Misguided Search for the Constitutional Definition of 'Religion,'" *Georgetown Law Journal* 71 (1983): 1564; Kent Greenawalt, "Religion as a Concept in Constitutional Law," *California Law Review* 72 (1984): 753–816; and J. P. Kuhn, "The Religious Difference: Equal Protection and the Accommodation of (Non)-

Religion," *Washington University Law Review* 94 (2016): 195–234. See also Brian Barry, *Culture and Equality* (Cambridge, MA: Harvard University Press, 2001) (arguing that religious preferences cannot be distinguished from expensive tastes).

20. Rawls defined a comprehensive doctrine as a moral conception that includes understandings "of what is of value in human life, and ideals of personal character, as well as ideals of friendship and of familial and associational relationships, and much else that is to inform our conduct, and in the limit to our life as a whole." John Rawls, *Political Liberalism* (New York: Columbia University Press, 1993), 13. Rawls believed that liberal society could never overcome the interminable disagreement that flowed from incommensurable comprehensive doctrines. Ibid., 224. But he maintained that we could still achieve political stability beyond a "modus vivendi" by constraining the dialogue between citizens through the concept of public reason. Ibid., 148. To this end, Rawls advocated that a "political conception" of justice could be attained "without reference" to comprehensive doctrines. Ibid., 12. Rawls later clarified that public reason "still allows us to introduce into political discussion at any time our comprehensive doctrine, religious or nonreligious, provided that, in due course, we give properly public reasons to support the principles and policies our comprehensive doctrine is said to support." John Rawls, "The Idea of Public Reason Revisited," *University of Chicago Law Review* 64 (1997): 776.

21. See generally, Rawls, *Political Liberalism*.

22. See generally, Rawls, "Idea of Public Reason Revisited."

23. Rawls insisted that on matters subject to public reason, "we are to appeal only to presently accepted general beliefs and forms of reasoning found in common sense, and the methods and conclusions of science when these are not controversial." John Rawls, *Theory of Justice* (Cambridge, MA: Harvard University Press, 1971), 224. Because public reason applies to citizens when they vote, "what public reason asks is that citizens be able to explain their vote to one another in terms of a reasonable balance of public political values." Ibid., 243. As I have suggested elsewhere, this premise requires us to embrace the fiction "that large segments of the population engage in a series of coherent argumentative steps to reach informed and intellectually defensible positions on a host of complex matters ranging from health care to foreign policy to medical ethics." John D. Inazu, "The Limits of Integrity," *Law and Contemporary Problems* 75 (2012): 185n33.

24. I use the phrase "modest unity" in *Confident Pluralism* to describe the conditions that allow us "to coexist in political community rather than in anarchy." Inazu, *Confident Pluralism*, 8.

25. Paul Kahn, *Political Theology: Four New Chapters on the Concept of Sovereignty* (New York: Columbia University Press, 2011), 23. Kahn observes, "When modern revolutionaries took up the task of translating the felt meaning of political revolution into a constitutional order of law, they thought of themselves as men of the Enlightenment using the language of reason to push religion out of the public sphere. This hardly means that they neither experienced nor relied upon

the sacred." Ibid. See also Stanley Fish, *There's No Such Thing as Free Speech, and It's a Good Thing, Too* (New York: Oxford University Press, 1994), 135:

> What if reason or rationality itself rests on belief? Then it would be the case that the opposition between reason and belief was a false one, and that every situation of contest should be recharacterized as a quarrel between two sets of belief with no possibility of recourse to a mode of deliberation that was not itself an extension of belief. This is in fact my view of the matter and I would defend it by asking a question that the ideology of reason must repress: where do reasons come from? The liberal answer must be that reasons come from nowhere, that they reflect the structure of the universe or at least of the human brain; but in fact reasons always come from somewhere, and the somewhere they come from is precisely the realm to which they are (rhetorically) opposed, the realm of particular (angled, partisan, biased) assumptions and agendas.

26. Trunk v. City of San Diego, 568 F. Supp. 2d 1199, 1218 (S.D. Cal. 2008), rev'd, 629 F.3d 1099 (9th Cir. 2011).

27. This blurring of religious and national symbolism is pervasive in American civic religion. For a critique of this kind of conflation, see, e.g., Stanley Hauerwas, *Christian Existence Today: Essays on Church, World and Living in Between* (Durham, NC: Labyrinth, 1988).

28. I explore the origins of the constitutional right of assembly in greater detail in John D. Inazu, *Liberty's Refuge: The Forgotten Freedom of Assembly* (New Haven, CT: Yale University Press, 2012).

29. Ibid., 22.

30. Ibid.

31. Ibid.

32. 494 U.S. 872 (1990).

33. The Supreme Court will still apply heightened scrutiny to a law or regulation that singles out religious belief or conduct for discriminatory treatment. See *Lukumi Babalu Aye, Inc. v. Hialeah*, 508 U.S. 520 (1993). But discriminatory intent is notoriously difficult to prove, and most laws that burden religion are neutral laws of general applicability that satisfy the *Smith* standard.

34. See the annual *State of the First Amendment* reports of the Newseum Institute available at http://www.newseuminstitute.org/first-amendment-center /state-of-the-first-amendment/.

35. Some of the last cases to address the right of assembly were *Edwards v. South Carolina*, 372 U.S. 229 (1963); *Cox v. Louisiana*, 379 U.S. 536 (1965); *Brown v. Louisiana*, 383 U.S. 131 (1966); *Shuttlesworth v. City of Birmingham*, 394 U.S. 147 (1969); and *Gregory v. City of Chicago*, 394 U.S. 111 (1969).

36. The right of association does not appear in the text of the Constitution. The Supreme Court first recognized it as implicit in the rights of speech and assembly

in *NAACP v. Alabama*, 357 U.S. 449 (1958). Twenty-six years later, the Court identified two separate constitutional sources for the right of association in *Roberts v. United States Jaycees*, 468 U.S. 609 (1984). Reviewing the cases that had emerged since *NAACP v. Alabama*, the *Jaycees* opinion found one line of decisions that protected "intimate association" as "a fundamental element of personal liberty." Another set of decisions guarded "expressive association," which was "a right to associate for the purpose of engaging in those activities protected by the First Amendment—speech, assembly, petition for the redress of grievances, and the exercise of religion" (*Jaycees*, 617–18).

37. The Court's speech-based focus in public forum cases included a group of decisions about time, place, and manner restrictions in a line of cases leading up to *Perry Education Ass'n v. Perry Local Educators' Ass'n*, 460 U.S. 37, 45 (1983). The implications of the speech-based focus of *Perry* can be seen in the Court's 1988 opinion in *Boos v. Barry*, 485 U.S. 312, 312–13 (1988). The case involved a challenge to a District of Columbia law that prohibited, among other things, congregating "within 500 feet of any building or premises within the District of Columbia used or occupied by any foreign government or its representative or representatives as an embassy, legation, consulate, or for other official purposes." Ibid., 316. The petitioners challenged the "deprivation of First Amendment speech and assembly rights" and argued that "the right to congregate is a component part of the 'right of the people peaceably to assemble' guaranteed by the First Amendment." Brief for Petitioners, Boos, 485 U.S. 312 (No. 86-803), 1987 WL 881333, at *36, *42. Justice Sandra Day O'Connor's opinion for the Court cited *Perry* three times and resolved the case under a free speech analysis without mentioning the right of assembly. *Boos*, 485 U.S. at 312–13, 317, 321, 324.

38. See *Roberts v. Jaycees*, 468 U.S. at 618 (defining expressive association as "a right to associate for the purpose of engaging in those activities protected by the First Amendment—speech, assembly, petition for the redress of grievances, and the exercise of religion").

39. Justice William Brennan observed that some bonds "foster diversity and act as critical buffers between the individual and the power of the State." *Roberts v. Jaycees*, 468 U.S. at 619. See also Richard W. Garnett, "The Story of Henry Adams's Soul: Education and the Expression of Associations," *Minnesota Law Review* 85 (2001): 1857 (our groups provide "alternative sources of meaning and education, and are essential both to genuine pluralism and to freedom of thought and belief"); and Kenneth L. Karst, "The Freedom of Intimate Association," *Yale Law Journal* 89 (1980): 688 ("One of the points of any freedom of association must be to let people make their own definitions of community").

40. I discuss this example in *Confident Pluralism*, 39–41.

41. Truth v. Kent. Sch. Dist., 542 F.3d 634, 645 (9th Cir. 2008). See also *Alpha Delta Chi–Delta Chapter v. Reed*, 648 F.3d 790, 795–96 (9th Cir. 2011) (suggesting that a public university could deny official recognition to Christian student groups

that limit "their members and officers [to those who] profess a specific religious belief, namely, Christianity").

42. In 1974, a federal appellate court upheld the associational rights of a gay student group against the University of New Hampshire's efforts to shut it down. Gay Students Org. of the Univ. of N.H. v. Bonner, 509 F.2d 652, 661 (1st Cir. 1974). In fact, "in an earlier era, public universities frequently attempted to bar gay rights groups from recognized student organization status on account of their supposed encouragement of what was then illegal behavior. The courts made short shrift of those policies." Brief for Petitioner at 30, Christian Legal Society v. Martinez, 561 U.S. 661 (2010) (No. 08-1371), 2010 WL 711183 2. Law professor Dale Carpenter has noted that "the rise of gay equality and public visibility coincided—not coincidentally, however—with the rise of vigorous protection for First Amendment freedom, especially the freedom of association." Dale Carpenter, "Expressive Association and Anti-discrimination Law after *Dale*: A Tripartite Approach," *Minnesota Law Review* 85 (2001): 1532–33. See also Lawrence A. Wilson and Rafael Shannon, "Homosexual Organizations and the Right of Association," *Hastings Law Journal* 30 (1979): 1046–62.

43. Nancy L. Rosenblum, *Membership and Morals: The Personal Uses of Pluralism in America* (Princeton, NJ: Princeton University Press, 1998), 36. See also *Boy Scouts of America v. Dale*, 530 U.S. 640, 647–48 (2000) (finding that freedom of association is "crucial in preventing the majority from imposing its views on groups that would rather express other, perhaps unpopular, ideas").

44. See generally, Alasdair MacIntyre, *After Virtue* (South Bend, IN: University of Notre Dame Press, 1981). As an example, consider MacIntyre's account of the "preliberal modern university." See Alasdair MacIntyre, *Three Rival Versions of Moral Enquiry: Encyclopedia, Genealogy, and Tradition* (South Bend, IN: University of Notre Dame Press, 1990), 230–32. MacIntyre envisions "the university as a place of constrained disagreement, of imposed participation in conflict, in which a central responsibility of higher education would be to initiate students into conflict." Ibid., 230–31. This would require participants "to enter into controversy with other rival standpoints, doing so both in order to exhibit what is mistaken in that rival standpoint in the light of the understanding afforded one's own point of view and in order to test and retest the central theses advanced from one's own point of view against the strongest possible objections to them to be derived from one's opponents." Ibid., 231.

45. John Inazu and Timothy Keller, "How Christians Can Bear Gospel Witness in an Anxious Age," *Christianity Today*, June 20, 2016:

> Today's cultural climate makes it especially essential for Christians to defend the religious liberty of American Muslims. Whatever challenges Christians may feel to their practices pale in comparison to the cultural and often legal challenges that confront American Muslims. As one Muslim leader shared, "Muslims today are afraid to

think in this country." These challenges are exacerbated when some Muslims engage in acts of terror in this country. Even though Christians and atheists also perpetrate acts of terror and violence (in places like movie theatres, elementary schools, and shopping malls), many of our neighbors react with particular fear and judgment when the perpetrator is identified with Islam.

46. See *Holt v. Hobbs*, 574 U.S. ___ (2015) (unanimous decision upholding the right of a Muslim prisoner under the Religious Land Use and Institutionalized Persons Act of 2000 to grow a half-inch beard despite an Arkansas prison regulation banning facial hair in most circumstances). See also Eugene Volokh, "*Holt v. Hobbs*: Unanimous Victory for Muslim Prisoner in Religious Rights Case," *Volokh Conspiracy*, January 20, 2015 (noting the Becket Fund's representation of the Muslim prisoner).

47. See, e.g., Russell Moore, "Why Christians Must Speak Out against Donald Trump's Muslim Remarks," *Washington Post*, December 8, 2015. ("As an evangelical Christian, I could not disagree more strongly with Islam. I believe that salvation comes only through union with Jesus Christ, received through faith. As part of the church's mission, we believe we should seek to persuade our Muslim neighbors of the goodness and truth of the gospel. It is not in spite of our gospel conviction, but precisely because of it, that we should stand for religious liberty for everyone.")

48. Charles Taylor, "Conditions of an Unforced Consensus on Human Rights," in *Dilemmas and Connections* (Cambridge, MA: Belknap Press of Harvard University Press, 2011), 105. See also Rawls, *Political Liberalism*; and Rebecca L. Brown, "Common Good and Common Ground: The Inevitability of Fundamental Disagreement," *University of Chicago Law Review* 81 (2014): 399 (the terrain of Rawls's overlapping consensus "must remain quite thin").

49. John Inazu, "We Disagree on the 'Self-Evident Truths' in the Declaration of Independence. But We Always Did," *Washington Post*, July 5, 2016.

50. Ibid.

51. I have explored the relationship between confident pluralism and Christian hope in a few shorter pieces. See, e.g., John Inazu, "Pluralism Doesn't Mean Relativism," *Christianity Today*, April 6, 2015; and Inazu and Keller, "How Christians Can Bear." One can find similar themes in the writings of theologian Lesslie Newbigin. See, e.g., Lesslie Newbigin, *Proper Confidence: Faith, Doubt, and Certainty in Christian Discipleship* (Grand Rapids, MI: Wm. B. Eerdmans, 1995).

Chapter 10: Plural America Needs Myths

1. See, among other venues, her essays in Diana Eck, *On Common Ground: World Religions in America* (New York: Columbia University Press, 2002).

2. Gananath Obeyesekere, *The Work of Culture: Symbolic Transformation in Psychoanalysis and Anthropology* (Chicago: University of Chicago Press, 1990).

3. Tvetan Todorov, *Symbolism and Interpretation* (Ithaca, NY: Cornell University Press, 1982), 32ff.

4. Wendy Doniger, *Other People's Myths: The Cave of Echoes* (New York: Macmillan, 1988; Chicago: University of Chicago Press, 1995), 146. Citations refer to the 1995 edition. Also see Wendy Doniger, *The Implied Spider: Politics and Theology in Myth* (New York: Columbia University Press, 1999).

5. Jonathan Sacks, *The Dignity of Difference* (New York: Continuum, 2002).

6. Laurie L. Patton, "The Doorkeeper, the Choirboy, and the Singer of Psalms: Notes on Narratives of Pragmatic Pluralism in the Twenty First Century," in *Interreligious Hermeneutics*, ed. Catherine Cornille and Christopher Conway (Eugene, OR: Wipf and Stock, 2010), 228–51.

7. Michele Lee Kozimor-King, "Interfaith Leadership and Sociology: An Interview with Eboo Patel," *Footnotes: A publication of the American Sociological Association*, accessed April 2, 2018, http://www.asanet.org/news-events /footnotes/jan-feb-mar-2017/features/interfaith-leadership-and-sociology -interview-eboo-patel.

8. Jean-Francois Lyotard, *The Postmodern Condition: A Report on Knowledge* (Minneapolis: University of Minnesota Press, 1979).

9. Virgil Nemoianu and Robert Royal, *The Hospitable Canon: Essays on Literary Play, Scholarly Choice, and Popular Pressures* (Amsterdam: John Benjamins, 1991). I am grateful to Tom Long at Emory University for this insight.

10. Diana Eck, *A New Religious America: How a "Christian Country" Has Become the World's Most Religiously Diverse Nation* (New York: HarperCollins, 2002), 11.

11. Pascal Boyer, *The Naturalness of Religious Ideas* (Berkeley: University of California Press, 1994); Robert McCauley and Thomas Lawson, *Bringing Ritual to Mind* (Cambridge: Cambridge University Press, 2002). Also see M. A. Upal, "An Alternative View of the Minimal Counterintuitiveness Effect," *Journal of Cognitive Systems Research* 11, no. 2 (2010): 194–203; Pascal Boyer and Charles Ramble, "Cognitive Templates for Religious Concepts," *Cognitive Science* 25 (2001): 535–64; and Justin L. Barrett and Melanie A. Nyhof, "Spreading Non-natural Concepts: The Role of Intuitive Conceptual Structures in Memory and Transmission of Cultural Materials," *Journal of Cognition and Culture* 1 (2001): 69–100.

12. The Four Chaplains Memorial Foundation, "The Story," accessed July 2, 2017, http://www.fourchaplains.org/the-saga-of-the-four-chaplains/.

13. Bruce Lincoln, "Mythic Narrative and Cultural Diversity in American Society," in *Myth and Method*, ed. Wendy Doniger and Laurie Patton (Charlottesville: University of Virginia Press, 1996), 163–77.

14. Ashutosh Varshney, *Ethnic Conflict and Civic Life* (New Haven, CT: Yale University Press, 2002).

15. Organization for Economic Cooperation and Development, *OECD Insights: Human Capital*, accessed July 4, 2017, https://www.oecd.org/insights /37966934.pdf.

16. Personal conversation with author, May 1, 2002, Atlanta, GA.

17. Varshney, *Ethnic Conflict and Civic Life.*

18. Andrea Cantor, "Jews Hand Muslims Synagogue Keys When a Texas Mosque Burns Down," *Forward,* January 31, 2017, http://forward.com/news /361793/jews-hand-muslims-synagogue-keys-when-a-texas-mosque-burns-down/.

19. Katherine Bindley, "Open Arms at an Unexpected Haven," *New York Times,* December 5, 2008, http://www.nytimes.com/2008/12/07/nyregion/thecity /07musl.html.

20. Ibid.

21. Jane Gross, "A Nation Challenged: Stretching a Jewish Vigil for the Sept. 11 Dead," *New York Times,* November 6, 2001, http://www.nytimes.com/2001/11 /06/nyregion/a-nation-challenged-vigil-stretching-a-jewish-vigil-for-the-sept-11 -dead.html.

22. Greater Lansing Chevra Kadisha, "A Summary of Jewish Practices in Death and Mourning," Kehillat Israel, April 2007, http://kehillatisrael.net/docs/chevra _summary.htm.

23. Gross, "Nation Challenged."

24. James L. Fredericks, introduction to *The New Comparative Theology: Interreligious Insights from the Next Generation,* ed. Francis X. Clooney (New York: Continuum Books, 2010), x–xviii.

Index

Abd-Allah, Umar, 105–6
Abdullah, Zaid, 94
Abedin, Huma, 45
abortion, 88
acceptance, movements for, 41
ACT for America, 53
action, exemplary, 158–59
Adams, John, 5
Addams, Jane, 27
advisers, Islamophobic, 52–55
African American Christians, 116
African American experience, connections
    to Islam, 98
African Americans, 9–10; black expressive
    culture, 97; Jews, 100–101. *See also*
    Muslims, African American; Muslims,
    American
Ahmadis, 93
Al Homssi, Amer, 60
Al-Andalus, 34
Ali, Mahershala, 93
Ali, Muhammad, 28, 75–77, 98
Allen, Danielle, xvi, 20, 28, 29
Althusius, Johannes, 26
alt-right, 54–55
America: Catholic experiences in, 105; as
    Judeo-Christian nation, 43; link with
    Islam, 34; Muslim experience in, 105;
    new stories about, 178–79; Protestant
    definition of, 69
American Academy of Family Physicians,
    61
American Covenant (Gorski), 23, 162–63
American dream tax, 109
American Enterprise Institute, 37
American Grace (Putnam and Campbell),
    14, 15, 22–23, 119

American Muslims. *See* Muslims, African
    American; Muslims, American;
    Muslims, immigrant
Americanness: Islamophobia and, 11–12;
    need to prove, 97; of religious
    communities, 8. *See also* identity,
    American
Andalusia, medieval, 34
Ansari, Aziz, 80–82, 83, 84, 85
Antepli, Abdullah, 65
anti-Catholicism, 22, 31–32, 42,
    105; Monk, 67–68; in politics, 67;
    positive pluralist response to, 7;
    similarity to anti-Muslim movement,
    66, 68
Anti-Defamation League, 64
anti-Muslim atmosphere, 7
anti-Muslim caucus, 45
anti-Muslim civil society, 55–59
anti-Muslim movement: ACT for America,
    53; growth of, 56; similarity to
    anti-Catholic movement, 66, 68;
    support for, 7; tropes of, 38
anti-Muslim narrative, 48–51
anti-Semitism, 64, 65, 79–80
anti-Shariah activists, 46
arrival, 159–160
assembly, right of, 142–43, 146
assimilation, xiv, xvi, 115, 126, 148
Associated Press–NORC poll, 122
association, art of, 14
association, right of, 143–46. *See also* First
    Amendment
Atlantic, The, 53, 120
audacity of equality, 109
authenticity, 10–11. *See also* Americanness
authority, sources of, 85

Democrats: civil rights movement and, 122; perceptions of discrimination, 123

demographic change, 118

denationalization, attempts at, 66, 68

DePaul University, 29

"Destroying the Great Satan: The Rise of Islamic Facism [sic] in America" (Bannon), 54

diaspora communities, 9. *See also* Muslims, immigrant

difference, dignity of, 155–56, 163

difference: maintenance of, 167–69; need for myths, 155; reinforcing, 133; value in, xii

disaffiliation, 118–19. *See also* unaffiliated, religiously

discrimination: against identity group, 60; perceptions of, 123; prevention of contributions by, 162–63

discriminatory policies. *See* policy

displacement, white Christian, xiv–xv, 120–21

dissent, as sacrilegious, 139

dissenters, 27–28

diversity, 7; acceptance of, 115; challenges in building, 16–20; challenges in dealing with, 22; change in dynamics of, 73–77; colleges and, 28–32; as compelling interest, 12–15; democracy and, 3; expectations of conformity and, 121; freedom and, 39–40; increasing, xiii; leveraging for common good, 3–4; within Muslim community, 9; vs. pluralism, xvi, 20, 152; relation to inequality, 12; reliance on melting pot idea, 115; responses to, 121–24; as strength, 6; threat to communities, 18; tolerance for in civic life, xiii–xiv; unhealthy, 21–22; use of term, 20; weaponized in partisan politics, 124. *See also* pluralism

Doniger, Wendy, 153

Dorchester, USS, 71, 153. *See also* Four Chaplains narrative

dream tax, American, 109

Dreher, Rod, 134

Duke, David, xx, 55, 56

Duke University, 65

E pluribus unum, xi–xiii, 18, 20, 124

Eck, Diana, 20, 152, 157, 167

Eid al Adha, 17

election (2016), 120, 121, 124. *See also* Trump, Donald

Ellison, Keith, 8, 10–11, 72, 75

El-Messidi, Tarek, 65

Emanuel African Methodist Episcopal Church, xii

Employment Division v. Smith, 141–42

equality: in American creed, 125; audacity of, 109

Erickson, Naomi, 173

Establishment Clause, 136–37, 139

ethics, everyday, xviii, 155–57

ethics, in foundational narratives, 177

Ethics after Babel (Stout), 130

ethnicity, class differences and, 11

evangelicals, 118

Evans, Hiram Wesley, 66–67

Evans, Janet, 76

exemptions, 137–38

expression, freedom of, 40, 41

expressive association, 143–46

extremism, 18; approaches to countering, 53; grants to fight, 59. *See also* terrorism

Fairey, Shepard, 86

faith, 4. *See also* religion

faith communities, 14. *See also* religious communities

Falwell, Jerry Jr., 148

Farsad, Negin, 92

Federalist Papers (Madison), 5

Feldman, Noah, 64

Fiddler on the Roof (film), 108

Fields, James Alex, 55

First Amendment, 12, 39; debates over, 140–41; Establishment Clause, 136–37, 139; Muslims and, 36–37; understandings of, 141–42. *See also* assembly, right of; association, right of; religion, freedom of

first responders, on 9/11, 40

OUR COMPELLING INTERESTS

Marta Tienda, Maurice P. During '22 Professor, Demographic Studies, & Professor, Sociology & Public Affairs, Princeton University

Sarah E. Turner, Chair, Department of Economics, University of Virginia

Internal Advisory Board

Saleem Badat, Program Director, AWMF

Armando I. Bengochea, Program Officer, AWMF

Nancy Cantor, Co-chair, Chancellor, Rutgers University-Newark

Makeba Morgan Hill, Deputy to the President and Chief Planner, AWMF

Earl Lewis, Co-chair, former President and Professor, AWMF, University of Michigan

Doreen N. Tinajero, Program Associate and Project Manager, AWMF

Eugene M. Tobin, Senior Program Officer, AWMF

Laura Washington, Director of Communications, AWMF

Michele S. Warman, Vice President, General Counsel and Secretary, AWMF

Mariët Westermann, Executive Vice President, AWMF